The Orthodox Church in
RUSSIA

The Orthodox Church in
RUSSIA
A Millennial Celebration

photographs by
Fred Mayer

texts by
Archbishop Pitirim of Volokolamsk
Archimandrite Longin of Düsseldorf
Leonid Uspensky
Bishop Serafim of Zurich
V. Feodorov

The Vendome Press
New York Paris

THIS BOOK HAS BEEN PRODUCED BY SPECIAL ARRANGEMENT WITH THE PATRIARCHATE OF
MOSCOW AND THE SOVIET AUTHORITIES, UNDER THE EDITORSHIP OF ARCHBISHOP PITIRIM
OF VOLOKOLAMSK, DIRECTOR OF THE PUBLISHING HOUSE OF THE JOURNAL OF THE MOSCOW
PATRIARCHATE.

Translated by Michael M. Wolyniec
Designed by Marlene Rothkin Vine

First published 1982 in Great Britain
by Thames and Hudson Ltd., London

Published in the United States of America
by The Vendome Press, 515 Madison Avenue, New York, N.Y. 10022
Distributed in the United States of America
by The Viking Press, 625 Madison Avenue, New York, N.Y. 10022
Distributed in Canada by Methuen Publishing Company

Library of Congress Cataloging in Publication Data
Mayer, Fred, 1933–
    The Orthodox Church of Russia.
    1. Russkaia pravoslavnaia tserkov'.   II. Pitirim,
Archbishop of Volokolamsk.   II. Title.
BX510.M39   281.9′3   82–6933
                                AACR2
ISBN 0-86565-029-2
Printed and bound in Switzerland
by Orell Füssli Graphische Betriebe AG, Zurich

Contents

1 The Trinity—Saint Sergiy Lavra ("Lavra" being the honorary title of a major monastery) at Zagorsk, 70 kilometers from Moscow, contains the grave of Saint Sergiy of Radonezh. On Pentecost, the patron feast of the Trinity—Saint Sergiy Lavra, thousands of pilgrims fill the churches and the great courtyard of the main monastery. His Holiness, Pimin, Patriarch of Moscow and All Russia, greets the faithful from the balcony of his patriarchal suite.

2 The Patriarch, accompanied by subdeacons, leaves the great church at Trinity—Saint Sergiy Lavra after the Pentecost service and returns to his suite.

3 During the liturgy in the cathedral at Trinity—Saint Sergiy Lavra, Patriarch Pimin, seated on his raised throne in the apse of the sanctuary, blesses one of the deacons before he reads from the Acts of the Apostles.

4 "The mercy of Our Lord Jesus Christ and of God the Father and of the community of the Holy Ghost be with you!" Patriarch Pimin sings at the beginning of the high service on Pentecost and blesses the faithful with three- and two-branched candelabra, the *Tririkon* (symbol of the Trinity) and the *Dirikon* (a reminder of Christ's twofold human and divine nature).

5 Patriarch Pimin is simultaneously Bishop of the diocese of Moscow and First Hierarch of the Russian Orthodox Church. More than a hundred times a year he celebrates the liturgy with his flock in the patriarchal Cathedral of Theopies in Moscow, in other churches of the capital, and in the Trinity—Saint Sergiy Lavra, of which he, as Archabbot, is also the head. The picture here shows the Moscow church that is dedicated to Saint Pimin the Great. Traditionally, Patriarch Pimin celebrates the liturgy in this shrine on his name day, August 27 (as indicated by the Julian calendar, which in our time lags thirteen days behind the Gregorian calendar followed in the West).

6 A banquet in 1980 on Patriarch Pimin's name day in Moscow's Sovetskaya Restaurant. The guests are Bishops, priests, and government officials.

7 Most of the faithful wait until the end of the service for the Patriarch to leave the church. Then as they thank His Holiness once more for his prayers and for the liturgy, they receive a further blessing.

Archbishop Pitirim of Volokolamsk

THE RUSSIAN ORTHODOX CHURCH
Ten Centuries of History and Culture

The greatest event in the history of the Russian land and its people occurred after almost a thousand years of preparation. In the middle of the 1st century, the Holy Apostle Andrew the First Called (d. A.D. 62) traveled across the immense East European plain from the southern to the northern seas, blessing and teaching as he went. According to Origen, he "had got as his lot Scythian land" and thus arrived by ship at Khersones. There he made contact with the Greek colonies of Taurida and established Christian communities that by the beginning of the 2nd century would number some two thousand members. Legend holds that as the Apostle advanced farther along the inland waterways to the Baltic, he foresaw, in the sparsely populated hills of the Dnieper region, the great churches and monasteries of Kiev, those holy shrines of the yet-unborn Rus. Evidence proving the existence of proto-Christian churches in the land of the Azov-Taurida tribes, before the devastating invasions of the Goths (mid-3rd century A.D.), has recently been discovered in the form of stone altars, church implements, and clay seals for making communion bread, all of which archaeologists date to the 1st century A.D. The Russian Orthodox Church, moreover, includes among the first few saints to shine forth in the Russian land the seven Bishops of Khersones who were martyred during the persecutions of Diocletian (4th century). And the Slavonic-speaking Tauro-Scythians, those forebears of the Russians that the Greeks called *Russi,* became the first among many tribes of the Rus territory to accept Christianity, doing so in the 6th and 7th

centuries and in great numbers. Meanwhile, they also accepted the Greek alphabet, which served as the basis of a proto-Russian script. Then in the second half of the 8th century came John the Goth, a Tauro-Scythian by birth who was consecrated Bishop and went on to participate in the Seventh Ecumenical Council. Some historians consider him to have been the first to translate the Holy Scripture into the Ruthenian tongue. It was also in Khersones that a century later, in 861, Saint Cyril, the Enlightener of the Slavs, discovered a Psalter and an Evangeliary written "in Russian characters" and was taught the language by one of the Ruthenians. The Cyrillic alphabet did not arrive in Kiev until the 10th century, conveyed there by a Bulgarian clergyman, but numerous manuscripts recounting the "Life of Saint Cyril" indicate that, once planted, this alphabet did not sprout from barren soil.

Slavs were first baptized in Kiev under Patriarch Photius in 867, and those so blessed included Princess Askold and Dir, along with some of their warriors and common people. The same year saw the establishment in Kiev of the first Russian diocese, the sixty-first within the Patriarchate of Constantinople. At the end of the 9th century a wooden church dedicated to the Prophet Elijah was built at Podol, in the region of Kiev, on the banks of the Pochaina River near a colony of Christian Slavs from Khazaria. The Byzantine Emperor, Basil of Macedonia, sent the converts a set of Gospels and a Psalter, written "in Russian characters." But the new church received no further assistance, and in 822 the first Christian Princes were tortured to death by the pagan Varangians. A few decades later, however, the devout Princess Olga, who had been baptized at Constantinople in 955, built the Church of Saint Nicholas over the grave of Askold and the Church of the Holy Wisdom *(Hagia Sofia)* over the grave of Dir.

In order to preserve the political independence of Rus, Kievan Prince Vladimir, along with his warriors, accepted baptism at Korsun (Khersones) in 987. He then invited two local clerics—Anastasius and Joachim, both Russian by birth—to return with him, the one to be his confessor and the other to become Bishop of Novgorod. In 988 the entire city of Kiev was bapitzed, when a solemn procession with icons and banners formed at the Church of the Prophet Elijah and moved toward the banks of the Dnieper. On that great day "joy was seen throughout heaven and earth at the sight of so many souls being saved," in the words of the *Tale of Bygone Times (Povest Vremmenykh Let)*, an ancient Russian chronicle written in the late 11th or early 12th century. That same summer, Christian conversion claimed all the largest cities of Rus, while the first Russian dioceses were established in Novgorod, Rostov, Vladimir, and Belgorod.

That year of national baptism proved to be a turning point for Russian civilization, which now entered its epochal period of spiritual consciousness, a time when the seeds of Christian culture were being sown throughout the bramble-fretted soil of Eastern Europe. A diverse and disparate Slavic populace suddenly emerged as a people, a national community unified through God and possessed of a faith that by and large would determine the destiny of Russia.

Since the native understanding of universal harmony *(lada)*, including the notion of the indivisibility of beauty, truth, and goodness, is deeply ingrained in the Indo-European consciousness, the view of the world held by ancient Rus was compatible with that of early Christianity. The young Russian Orthodox Church had simply to reveal to the people the Christian fullness present in the Holy Trinity, declaring that Divine Truth can exist only in mystical union with Beauty and Goodness.

By introducing this notion of Higher Beauty, Orthodoxy penetrated the very heart of the Russian character. From the wealth of literature produced by Kievan Rus, only a few fragments survive, but these include the *Sermon on Law and Grace*, composed in the 1040s by the Metropolitan Ilarion (d. 1088), a leading writer and thinker of the 11th-century Rus; Saint Nestor's *Tale of Bygone Times*, one of the most important European chronicles of this historic period; the *Lives of the Fathers of the Kiev-Pechery Lavra (Paterik)*, written at the end of the 12th and the beginning of the 13th century by the monks Simon and Polikarp; the *Sermons* and *Epistles* of Cyril, Bishop of Turov (d. 1183); the *Supplication of Saint Daniil* (late 12th–early 13th century), who exemplified the best traditions of Byzantine oratory; the fervently nationalistic *Pilgrimage of Abbot Daniil*, an early 12th-century account of a journey to Palestine; and, of course, the famous *Lay of Igor's Campaign (Slovo o polku Igoreve)*, written in 1187. Such works became a nucleus not only for the swift emergence of a distinctive Kievan Rus literature, but also for the medieval Russian literature that would develop in the next century. Even today they reveal the reverential wonder with which the first generation of Russian Christians embraced their environment, as well as the vast and transforming influence that the new literary culture exerted upon native folklore. The *bylinny*, or warrior sagas, the epic tales, folk songs, fables, proverbs, and the subsequent spiritual verse of the numerous pilgrims and wandering folksingers evince such a joyous spirit of Christianity that the heavens and the earth would seem to have been transformed and the very land christened and sanctified along with the people inhabiting it.

The immense, creative energy of the new Christian faith—indeed the dominant cultural role played by the Russian Orthodox Church—constituted a major factor in the history of Kievan Rus. Liturgy unfolded in a language completely familiar to the people, who congregated at the nearly ten thousand churches and some two hundred monasteries that came into being from the 11th to the 13th century. According to the chronicles, Kiev alone lost seven hundred churches to the great fire of 1124. It has been estimated that no less than one hundred thousand manuscript books were in circulation at this time, most of them originating in Bulgaria, Serbia, and Athos. Among the schools constructed during the period, one of the largest—with a five-hundred seat capacity—came from the patronage of the Kievan Prince Yaroslav the Wise (1019–54) in Novgorod. At Smolensk in the mid-12th century Prince Roman Rostislavich expended vast resources on school construction and maintenance, thereby gaining for that city the reputation of being, probably, the most literate of all Russian cities. At the beginning of the next century Grand Prince Vsevolod of Vladimir conceived such a zeal for education that he donated his own palace and a substantial portion of his personal fortune to the cause of enlightenment.

Birchbark documents discovered in the 1950s and 1960s bear witness to the general literacy that prevailed in these and other cities of ancient Rus. Simultaneously with the establishment of Catholic Europe's first universities in the 12th century, the soil of Old Russia began to sprout great monasteries, themselves true centers of learning. In this phenomenon lay one of the earliest manifestations of the difference between the "rationality" of Western culture and the "spirituality" of Eastern culture. The first Russian monestary was founded at Athos early in the 11th century. Then came the renowned "Monastery of the Caves" at Kiev, established in 1051 by Saint Antoniy, spiritual leader at Athos and the father of Russian monasticism. The glorious cloisters at Kiev provided spiritual nourishment for the first Russian miracle-workers, church hierarchs, elders, and learned men. They also constituted the most important center for spiritual instruction within the Russian Orthodox Church, a school of piety and Christian asceticism. The Russian calendar includes more than one hundred saints who were associated with the monastery at various times. The monasteries of medieval Russia had their own rules, and while these were, for the most part, severe, they did not govern the spiritual development or the charitable works of the communities' members. Special monastic orders, like those found in the Roman Catholic Church, did not exist in Rus.

The 11th and 12th centuries were also the period when the first examples of Russian religious art appeared: cathedrals styled in the luxurious Byzantine manner, as at the Saint Sofia churches in Kiev (1037), Novgorod (1050), and Polotsk (1066), as well as in the completely original stone churches at Vladimir, Suzdal, and Rostov, which rose decades later. A style of greater aesthetic restraint appeared during the 12th and 13th centuries at Pskov, Smolensk, and Staraja Lagoda. A few of the early Russian masters are actually known by name: the architects Mironeg and Nikolai Zhdan from Kiev (11th century); Iakov Korov of Novgorod (12th century); Pyotr Miloneg (late 12th–early 13th century) who built churches at Kiev, Smolensk, and Orvuch; the painters Blessed Alimpiy of the Monastery of the Caves (11th century); and the Novgorodian Aleksiy Petrov (13th century); the stonecutter Avdey from Galich (13th century); the skilled enameler Lazar Bogshi from Polotsk (12th century); and the Novgorodian engravers Flor Bratila and Konstantin (12th century).

Highly developed by this time was the art of calligraphy and manuscript illumination, which can be seen the richly decorated *Ostromirov Gospel* (1057), the *Anthology (Izbornik)* of Svyatoslav (1073), and the *Arkhangelsk Gospel* (1092).

Simultaneously with art and architecture, the first native Russian ecclesiastical music emerged in the 11th century, a product of interaction between Greek and Bulgaro-Serbian cultures and the Russian folk tradition. Important manifestations are the *Canons* (c. 1120) of Saint Grigoriy of Pechery and the *Prayers* to the first Holy Martyrs, Saints Boris and Gleb (1072), and to Saint Feodosiy of Pechery (1095).

Although new to ancient Russia, Christian culture flourished there as if it had been indigenous rather than foreign, thanks to the mediating role played by Balkan missionaries, whose Slavic culture had an affinity with that of Russia. Metropolitan Ilarion was convinced that the Russian Church, despite its youth, possessed "blessed equality" with the other Orthodox Churches. And the validity of this conviction is borne out by the mature and fully realized artistic forms that grew up spontaneously from the depths of Russian Christianity in the 11th, 12th, and 13th centuries.

At the time Rus underwent conversion, Byzantine society was experiencing a period of political and religious renewal. Once Byzantium had overcome the iconoclastic heresy in the 9th century, monasticism became a resurgent influence throughout the Greek Church. This meant that the Orthodoxy accepted by Rus had been purified through many tribulations and strengthened by the generous help of its many saints and its steadfast adherence to the patristic traditions. Still, theology and religious philosophy developed relatively late in Russian cultural history,

not until the 15th and 16th centuries, a fact explained by the stifling influence of the Tatar-Mongol Yoke (13th–15th centuries) as well as by the Russian people's acceptance of Orthodoxy as something concrete, moral, and alive. Thus, the forms of "practical theology" and "philosophical speculation" that proved most acceptable to the Christians of Ancient Rus were those of religious art, committed as this was to the creation of visible and audible representations of the celestial world. Russians conceived of Christianity as "the other life," meaning a monastic existence or an image of God's life *on earth*. Deep devotion joined with pure and passionate faith to lead both layman and monk to asceticism, that powerful, voluntary aspiration to high evangelical ideals.

These qualities, so providentially bestowed, helped the Russian people endure the difficult trials that would beset them for many centuries, either through long years of isolation from the European world, or in many a fierce struggle to survive, often against circumstances forced upon them by history.

From the very outset, every level of Russian society embraced Orthodox Christianity, a fact that enabled the Church to become a bulwark of early Russian statehood. Thus, the Byzantine concept of a "symphony" of temporal and spiritual authority provided the very foundation of the new political life of Rus. Ecclesiastical unity functioned as a prototype for political unity. Soon, however, the power of Orthodoxy to inspire and sustain the Russian spirit would be tested, for the death of Kievan Grand Prince Vladimir Monomakh in 1113 plunged the country into a drawn-out cycle of dynastic conflict that resulted in feudal dismemberment. This internecine process deepened for more than a century, only to conclude in a national disaster.

In 1237 the fragmented state of Kievan Rus suffered a crushing blow when it was overrun by hordes of Central Asian nomads. Once the strong state in Europe, Rus simply disintegrated under the impact of the massive invasion, and in 1240 the principalities of northeastern Russia, left untouched by the Asiatic tribes, found themselves subject to threat from the Swedes and the knights of the powerful Teutonic Order. This crusade, however, was turned back by troops under the command of the great Novgorodian Prince, Saint Aleksandr Nevsky, who took schema[1] before his death in 1263 and entered the ranks of saints as Patron of the Russian Land.

Throughout this period, "ruination of the Russian land" was all too often the lot of the Russian people, but with each new devastation the invocatory peal of the few church bells that remained would ring still louder, resounding over the ravaged cities and trampled fields.

The Mongol-Tatar Yoke lasted two hundred and fifty years, but while it subjected the Russian people to outrage and terror from foreign tyrants, it also provided a time for quietly developing and husbanding the nation's own internal strength. As in other, later times of war, starvation, and sudden impoverishment, the Orthodox monasteries experienced a significant influx of new converts to the religious life. What Russians heard from their Church was a ceaseless call for national penance and spiritual purification, a strict regimen of sacrifice from monks and novices, and a rejection of dynastic interests on the part of the great feudal lords, so that a humbled nation might rise from its knees. In 1299 the Metropolitan See was moved from Kiev to the city of Vladimir. Then, in 1325, Saint Peter, Metropolitan of All Russia from 1308 to 1326, moved it again, this time to Moscow, an unobtrusive wooded town lost somewhere in the forests of Central Rus. This set the stage for the gathering of the Russian lands and for a rebirth of the nation.

Consciously or unconsciously, the principle of Divine Administration (Russian: *domostroitel' stvo*; Greek: *oikonomia*) informed all political and ecclesiastical forces in Rus, forces that the Metropolitan Aleksiy (r. 1354–78) directed through his personal spiritual authority. By curing the Tatar Princess Taidula of blindness, he delivered the fledgling Muscovite principality from the destructive raids of the Golden Horde. For the advancement of spiritual instruction, to which he attached great importance, Aleksiy translated the New Testament from Greek into Russian. A tireless spokesman for national unity, he rallied the people round the Church, doing so in the very teeth of the terrible enemy. One of the great Metropolitan's pupils was Dimitriy Donskoi, the future Grand Prince of Muscovy.

In 1334, Saint Sergiy, one of the brilliant lights of Orthodoxy, established what would soon become a very great monastery in the forest outside Moscow near the small town of Radonezh. Shut off from the world, half hidden in the thick woods of Central Russia, this secluded monastery—the future Trinity–Saint Sergiy Lavra[2]—developed, through the ascetic prayer of its founder, into the spiritual center of the entire country. Moreover, Saint Sergiy of Radonezh found himself named, by the people themselves, "Hegumen of the Russian land." Monks and pilgrims, clerics and princes made the journey to the squalid cell that the holy man had built with his own hands. Here, before the Battle of Kulikovo (1380), perhaps the most important military engagement to occur in Eastern Europe during the Middle Ages, Dimitriy Donskoi arrived for the blessing of Sergiy, who foretold victory. As his assistants, Donskoi received two monks, whose armor consisted of faith and the prayers of their spiritual leader. The first monk, Aleksandr Peresvet, fell in hand-to-hand combat with an

---

[1] *Schema* (or "Great Schema") is the strictest form of Eastern monasticism.

[2] *Lavra* is the honorary title of a major monastery.

enemy warrior. Soon thereafter the second monk, Andrei Oslyabya, also forfeited his life for the liberation of Rus.

Still, a century would pass before the hated Yoke finally gave way in 1480. The trials that Rus underwent in the 13th, 14th, and 15th centuries coincided, both chronologically and thematically, with the Reconquista of Spain. In each country the struggle against foreign tyranny entailed untold suffering and privation for the oppressed people, yet it furthered the development of their massive spiritual strength. By the end of the 15th century, a humiliated and politically divided Rus was replaced by a more cohesive and independent nation: Russia.

In the 14th and 15th centuries both the old and the newly established monasteries became focal points for the spiritual revival of Russia. The entire woodland region of Northern Russia came alive with a network of large monastic settlements that attracted great numbers of peasants, who in turn peacefully cultivated this vast frontier, thereby helping the missionary and educational activity to continue unabated. Saint Stefan, Bishop of Perm (d. 1396), preached among the Komi people along the northern Dvina; he also created an alphabet for them and translated the Gospel into their language. Saints Sergiy and Yerman (d. 1353) established the Valaam Monastery of the Transfiguration of the Savior on the islands of Lake Lagoda and went forth to preach among the Karelian tribes. Saints Savva (d. 1438) and Zosima (d. 1478) laid the foundations for what was to be the greatest monastery in northern Europe, the Solovetsk Monastery of the Transfiguration of the Savior on the islands of the White Sea. Saint Cyril (d. 1427) initiated a monastery in the Belozersk region, while Saint Feodorit of Kola, at the beginning of the 16th century, converted the Finnish Lopari tribe and gave them an alphabet. His mission was continued by Saint Trifon of Pechenga (d. 1583), who founded a monastery on the northern shores of the Kola Peninsula.

The 250 years of the Mongol enslavement can justifiably be called medieval Russia's age of monasticism, the climactic moment of which occurred in the 15th century. The artistic culture of the period has been preserved in the icons of the painters Feofan the Greek (d. 1515), Saint Andrei Rublyov (c. 1360–1428), the older Prokhor of Gorodets (late 15th–early 16th century), the monk Daniil Chernyi (1360–1430), and Saint Dionisiys Glushitskiy (1362–1437). It also survives in the work of the Moscow Kremlin architect and sculptor Vasiliy Yermolon of Moscow (d. 1485), the skilled carver Amvrosiy, a monk of the Trinity–Saint Sergiy Lavra (1430–94), the monastic scribe Epifaniy the Wise (died c. 1420), and Luka "the Singer" (13th century) of Vladimir, an early Russian composer who initiated the tradition of Russian Church choral music. Despite its anonymity, this ever-deepening culture left an indelible mark everywhere in the land, and the era can safely be called a true epoch in the history of religious art. In an age of autonomous principalities, the Orthodox Church constituted the only institution capable of endowing Russian culture with a national character. Nowhere is the indigenous creativity of the period more evident than in the multilevel iconostasis and tent-roof mode of church construction, a genuine national style of architecture that first appeared in the northern regions.

In the middle of the 14th century came the "Hesychast" movement and with it a factor that would prove all important in the development of Russian culture during the next several decades. Originating at Athos and spread through the work of Saint Gregory of Sinai, Hesychasm searched endlessly for the "Kingdom of the Faithful," which would be revealed through a world transformed by Divine Saving Grace. Thus, the movement could only reinforce that inherent element in the Russian character which quests for a higher

"Beauty of Existence" and a "living faith." The continuous Reasonable Prayer of the Hesychast became a "ladder" to this kingdom, which proved to be "Holy Writ" and could be transformed into the mystical "Heavenly City." When filled with the highest quality of spiritual verse, the art of prayer was regarded as the most complete form of creativity available to human individuals. Indeed, the individual became the main object of prayer, with all else serving merely as preparation for the mystical union with God (Russian: *obozhenie*; Greek: *apotheiosis*). The mysticism surrounding the transformation to sainthood is a universal theme in Christianity, a theme that in Russian Orthodoxy is related to the reverence for Holy Relics, which the Hesychasts gave a new impetus. Thus, religious art developed in the bosom of Russian spirituality, right along with the emergence of monastic and lay asceticism. However, it was at the very moment of their apogee that artistic forms inspired by religion were subjected to the "sacred silence," which replaced the songs of the spirit with deep prayerful silence. A clear indication of this can be found in the long interruptions, yet unexplained, in the unusually intense "monastic" art of Saint Andrei Rublyov.

In 1453 came an event that shook the entire Christian world. After a long struggle, the city of Constantinople capitulated to the Muslim Turks, ending the thousand-year history of the Byzantine Empire. The Russian Orthodox Church had been autocephalous since 1448, a consequence of the Union of Florence (1453), whereby the Greek Church accepted the primacy of the Pope of Rome. Traditional Grecophilism, which grew from a Russian belief in the divine exclusivity of the Greek Church, now gave way to different feelings. This trend gained momentum during the "Joanine Era" (late 15th to late 16th century), a period coincident with that of Russia's national consolidation. By the beginning of the 16th

century, Russia had essentially become the only sovereign Orthodox state, whereas the Bulgarians, Rumanians, and Serbs had suffered the same fate as the Greeks, falling under a Turkish yoke that would not be lifted for four hundred years. Meanwhile, the lands of western and northern Russia submitted to the power of the Catholic Polish-Lithuanian Republic and the influence of the Uniate Church.

Altogether, the situation in Russia brought forth a new theory designed to guide the affairs of Church and State, in both their legal and their ecclesiastical aspects. Called "Moscow: the Third Rome," the concept is alleged to have been formulated by Filofey (1453–1528), Abbot of the Monastery of Saint Eleazar at Pskov, in a series of four letters to Tsar Vasily III and his deacon, Misiur-Munekhik, in the 1510s and 1520s. The notions of a divinely chosen people, the "wandering" Rome, and the preeminence of state power had wide circulation in Byzantium and had become well known in Russia by the end of the 15th century. What was new in the ideas of Filofey was his conviction that the Tsar should remain "sovereign," that is, independent, so as to enforce fidelity to Orthodoxy, which had saved the Russian nation from destruction. The Russian monarch was called upon to take political command of the entire Orthodox world, and to lead the struggle for its liberation from Catholic caesaropapism and Muslim theocracy. This belief, supported by subsequent Russian rulers, grew out of a sense that the Christian ministry entailed a responsibility toward the Universal (Catholic) Orthodox Church, not out of the religious fervor of "messianic nationalism," which has sometimes been seen as a fundamental, informing factor within the ideology of Muscovite Rus.

During these years the spirit of Russian Orthodoxy remained primarily one of "tutelage," meaning that the Russian Church graciously accepted Greeks, Bulgarians, Serbs, and refugees from other Orthodox Churches and sometimes invited them to give "literary instruction." These newly baptized Orthodox Christians were even called upon to occupy positions of authority in the Church hierarchy. The 17th-century Patriarch Nikon of Moscow and All Russia was a Modvinian. Some—such as Saint Pafnutiy Borovsky (15th century), a converted Tatar—would enter the ranks of the canonized.

By the second half of the 16th century, Filofey's proposals, directed as they were against Roman and Turkish hegemonism, had been accepted by all East Orthodox Patriarchs, and in 1589 the Russians, with great ceremony, established a Patriarchate in their own country. This formalized the latent but ever-growing spiritual power of the Russian Church and its authority in the Orthodox world. The first Patriarch of All Russia was Iov (1589–1606), the Metropolitan of Moscow.

After its victory over the Tatar khanates of Kazan (1552) and Astrakhan (1554), Russia advanced into the Asian continent, proselytizing among the numerous nomadic peoples of Siberia, while also promoting the gradual settlement and peaceful economic integration of the northern section of the vast Eurasian land mass. By this time the Russian Orthodox Church had received its first complete translation of the Bible into Slavonic, thanks to the efforts of many writers, translators, and scribes gathered at the Novgorod Episcopal See under the leadership of Bishop Gennadiy (d. 1505). And with the active distribution of the vernacular text among the largest monasteries, which also received a large body of other religious works, the network of monastic libraries destroyed by the Tatars underwent a vigorous revival.

Saint Iosif of Volokolamsk (1439–1515), a leading Church publicist, urged that the strict personal asceticism of the monk be combined with an all-inclusive "gathering"—both spiritual and material—of the larger monastic communities. Fortified with this principle, Saint Iosif and his followers (Iosifites) energetically defeated the heresies that emerged at the end of the 15th century, promoted construction of churches and monasteries, supported literacy and the artistic work of such icon painters as the great Dionisiys (d. 1505), and nurtured the growth of liturgical music. The tradition this established, with powerful backing from the Metropolitan Makariy of Moscow (1428–1563) and his supporters, heavily influenced the decisions of the Church Council of 1551. This council, which condemmed both heresy and the Uniate schism, can be compared to the Council of Trent (1545–65) through which the Roman Catholic Church initiated its Counter-Reformation.

Accompanying the Iosifite movement was another tradition within the Russian Orthodox Church, promoted by the so-called *nestyazhateli*, the self-proclaimed followers of Saint Nil Sorksy (1433–1508), a famed theologian who at the late-15th- and early-16th-centruy councils opposed the practice of *styazhanie* ("money grubbing"), or the active economic expansion of monasteries so forcefully advocated by Saint Iosif Volokolamsk and his followers. In his writings, Saint Nil confronted the Orthodox Church with the issue of the Hesychast heritage. A student and follower of Paisiys Yaroslavov, an elder from Athos, Saint Nil had gained his own priceless religious experience from the continuous "Jesus Prayer," the seclusion of monastic life, and total inner-directed silence. He tried to nurture in other monastics the sensation of "walking before God" and to instill the rules for renouncing worldly pursuits, all of which require constant effort. Saint Nil proposed that every monk follow the path of personal service to the nation's faithful, an approach that stood in opposition to the Iosifites, who required that monastic societies render ecclesiastical service to the state as a whole.

These two traditions—Isoifite and Nestyazhatel—supplement each other to a great extent. A powerful advocate of the former was the noted 16th-century philosopher and writer Zinoviy Otensky (d. 1568). The first in Russia to interpret the works of John of Damascus, Otensky published essays in the 1560s that undertook to do philosophical battle with the blatant atheism of such heretics as Matvei Bashkin and Feodisiy Kosoi, thereby providing original ontological and cosmological arguments for the existence of God. The "Old Believer" (*Starchestvo*) tradition that ensued is rooted in the works of Saint Nil. According to the Old Believers, the basic goal of Christian life is to nourish the people with bread and Scripture. For many centuries, these monastic traditionalists, sharing poverty and adversity with the common people, were considered the authentic conscience of the Russian nation.

One of the most striking and complex phenomena of Russian religious history is surely to be found in the spiritual kin of the *nestyazhateli* known as the *yurodivyi*, an untranslatable Russian word that corresponds to the Greek *hyperephanos*, meaning "fool for the sake of Christ" or "God's fool." Practically unknown to the Western Church, the "God's fools" have occasionally appeared in the Greek and Egyptian Churches, but they flourished in the Russian Church. Although the "fools" voluntarily renounced the rational world and engaged in "holy nonsense," they cannot be interpreted simply as exponents of the "extralogical act" (*opera superrogacionis*). What they did was doggedly pursue moral and social evil, and thus can be thought of as a kind of "spiritual knighthood" within the Orthodox world. Literature has produced something comparable in the characters of Don Quixote and Prince Myshkin. Their lives taken up with the fight against sin, the Russian "fools" fearlessly choose "to do battle with

the world," and from their peak of ascetic self-renunciation, they literally sacrifice themselves to the sins of their contemporaries, doing so in order to destroy or "transfigure" those sins. They enter the arena where the usual preaching, prayers, and charitable works have proved powerless, the better to save the prodigal, to return the thief or heretic to the fold. The Russian Church considered these people a special gift and called them "God's folk" (*bozhie liudy*). By the beginning of the 18th century, the "fools" no longer constituted a prominent feature of Russian religious and social life, but they never totally disappeared from the history of the Orthodox Church.

Come the middle of the 16th century, Russian culture began to exhibit undeniably distinctive traits of a completely national character. Artistic endeavor was devoted exclusively to ecclesiastical purposes. The political "gathering of the Rus," together with the extension of economic ties throughout all regions of the nation, fostered the country's cultural integration, but this did not diminish or eliminate the local characteristics of religious life, local chronicle traditions, or artistic schools. The Church's responsibility to the "eternal memory" of its heroes, like the Russian tradition of "commemorating," led to the introduction of many locally revered saints into the ranks of Russian sainthood at the Church councils of the mid-16th century and in later years. During this period, the body of literature on the lives of the saints multiplied, the great chronicles appeared, and the first achievements of the provincial schools of art flowed together and formed a unified Russian culture with its center in Moscow. The Church of the Ascension in the village of Kolomenskoye (1532), the oldest surviving example of Russian tent-roof architecture, reveals the influence of the wood architecture native to northern Russia. Clearly reflected in the art and architecture of the Kremlin's 15th- and 16th-century cathedrals are the prototypes provided by the churches of Rostov and the icon painting of Suzdal. In the late 16th century, simultaneously with the development of the "Godunov" style of monumental painting in Moscow, the "Stroganov" school of refined miniature script emerged in the provinces, a style superbly represented by the work of Prokopiy Churin (1580–1620), Istoma Savin, and his sons Nazariy and Nikifor (late 16th–early 17th century) from Solvychegodsk, and Emelian Moskvitin (17th century). The recently discovered *Pevcheskii sbornik* ("Song Collection"; 1557–58) of Elisei Vologzhanin contains the earliest known examples of liturgical vocal music, clearly and closely connected with the lyrical tradition of Russian song and the melodies and texts of "penitential verse." In the mid-16th century came an official state choir, formed of the finest professional singers in Moscow, and music made its first appearance in the Patriarchal service. But the greater part of Moscow's musical culture in the later part of the century would be unthinkable without the contributions of the Novgorodians Ivan Shaidur and Vasiliy Rogov, both noteworthy representatives of the *demestvennyi* ceremonial of Russian church music, and their students Fedor Khristianin of Moscow and Stefan Golysh, a native of far-off Usolie. Moscow was fast becoming a powerful cultural center, and under its influence, other artistic breeding grounds also began to develop, each with its own unique local peculiarities. This is especially true in the realm of 16th-century handicrafts: enamel, niello, and metal engraving. The period also saw the flowering of personalized embroidery, which produced those sumptuous yet delicate "women's icons." Noteworthy examples of this highly developed art form can be found in the unusually expressive burial shrouds and palls, stitched with gold, silver, and silk threads and modeled after the work of Princess Maria of Tver (late 14th–early 15th century), Princess Evfrosinia Stariskaya and her pupils, the Tsaritsa Anastasia, wife of Ivan the Terrible (mid-16th century), Princess Kseniya Godunova (late 16th–early 17th century), M.I. Stroganova (mid-17th century), and many anonymous masters of the northwestern monasteries.

Sculpture was never highly developed in Russian church art. The early Christians had regarded statues and relief carvings as a holdover from paganism, with the result that flatness of image became a canon of Byzantine art. The oldest surviving examples of Russian wood-carved sculpture—revered images of Saint Nicholas, the miracle-worker, Archbishop of Myra, and the Holy Martyr Saint George the Victorious slaying a dragon with his spear—date from the 14th century. Apart from these patrons of the Russian land, the most universally venerated images are those of Saint Parasceve and the Icon of the Mother of God, "Consolation of All the Afflicted." In the 17th and 18th centuries, wooden church sculpture appeared in western and northeastern Russia, expressing local artistic traditions but also reflecting exposure to the Western Baroque. Perm constructed an iconostasis of sculptured wood. In the following centuries crucifixes became common, along with the especially popular images of Christ sitting in prison. Carved miniature icons were also popular, often displaying the images of Saint Sergiy of Radonezh, Saint Serafim of Sarov, and also Saint Nil of Stolobny Island, a 16th-century hermit famous for his sacred pledge never to sit or lie down, or even to sleep.

At the outset of the 17th century the state-sponsored construction that had got off to such a vigorous start in the previous century suffered a setback, for now Russia entered the period forever etched on memories as the notorious "Time of Troubles." This was the bloody age of Ivan the Terrible (1530–84) and his infamous *oprichnina*.

When Ivan undertook to subject the Russian Church to his own personal rule, he so weakened the nation that it almost fell under a new foreign domination. Invasion by Polish-Lithuanians and Swedes, which destroyed half the country, exposed the weakness of the Russian autocracy. But it is precisely this political frailty that brought out the immense moral strength of the Russian people, who rallied round the Church, forming a national volunteer army for the defense of the nation and installing a new dynasty—that of the Romanovs (1613)—upon the shaky tsarist throne. Once again the forgotten Byzantine theory of the "symphony" of temporal and spiritual authority became official doctrine, a doctrine that assumed legitimacy as soon as the *Zemsky Sobor*, or "Great Council," convened with representatives from both Church and State. The Russian national consciousness will always keep alive the patriotism of those monks from the Trinity–Saint Sergiy Lavra who fought off a Polish siege for more than a year, thereby spiritually fortifying the population for battle, and that of Holy Martyr Germogen, a follower of the Orthodox faith and Patriarch of All Russia (1602–12), who sounded the cry for national liberation and died a martyr's death for his refusal to unite with Catholicism.

In 1654 the Ukraine reunited with Russia and returned the nation of ancient Rus to the Orthodox Church. The event also provided a religious, political, and military defense of Russia from the destructiveness of Polish-Lithuanian feudalism and the Uniate clerics. In 1596, by the Union of Brest, the Ukraine and Belorussia had seen their Orthodox Churches subordinated to the Vatican and their lands stripped of national and religious independence. In 1654–55 Russia fought Poland in the first war waged for the restoration of Ukrainian national rights and succeeded in incorporating Smolensk as well as other Russian lands into the main body of the Russian nation.

The religious culture of 17th-century Russia had to struggle not only against a foreign enemy but with internal evil as well. The Time of Troubles exposed a host of defects in Russian ecclesiastical life. Additional harm resulted from local differences in Church custom and ceremony. The Archimandrite Dionisiys (Zobnikovskiy, d. 1633) of the Trinity–Saint Sergiy Lavra was one of the first to recognize the necessity for putting religious life in order, for introducing greater literacy, and for strengthening national morality. Under his spiritual guidance, a group of clerics and laymen, the "circle of pious zealots," gathered in Moscow in the late 1640s to discuss internal Church reforms, with the Tsar Alexei Mikhailovich taking a keen interest in the proceedings. The circle included both the champion of liturgical reform, the holy Patriarch Nikon (1652–58), and his main rival, the religious spokesman and writer Archpriest Avvakum Petrov (1621–82), who led the traditionalist faction represented by the Old Believers.

The Church Councils of the 1650s and 1660s concerned themselves mainly with correcting liturgical books and customs, a process that provoked a crisis, since the traditionalist school could not be reconciled to it. What resulted was the Old Believer Schism, a schism that occured for reasons both religious and cultural. In the mid-17th century, the Iosifite tradition collided with traditional Orthodox devotion (*blagochestie*), or "piety". One extreme antagonized another. The more violent adherents to the old ways professed that they would rather die in a holy fire than submit to the decisions of the Russian Church Local Councils of the 1660s and 1670s or to those taken by the Council of Eastern Orthodox Partiarchs in the 1680s. The Old Believers essentially rejected the Church's attempt to reconcile two traditions. But the need for reconciliation had been first voiced in the 16th century by the famous writer and publicist

Maksim the Greek (d. 1556), the diplomat Feodor Karpov (d. 1545), the philosopher Zinoviy Otensky, and the learned writer Prince Andrei Kurbsky (1528–83), who argued brilliantly with Ivan the Terrible. Then in the 17th century came the admonitions of Dionysiys Troitsky and the "defenders of the faith." Not until 1971 did Russia revoke the oaths and anathemas laid down against the Old Believers in the Church Councils of 1656 and 1666–67. Thus, in the mid-17th century Russian Orthodoxy succeeded in overcoming its propensity to isolationism, a tendency that the Old Believers exemplified to an extreme degree. The new development permitted relations with Greek, Bulgarian, and Serbian clergy, as well as those with the Orthodox brotherhoods in western and southern Russia, to gain strength and deepen. The rich cultural experience of the fraternal Churches could not but have a beneficial effect on the Russian Church and the advancement of its religious education and culture. In 1649 the Boyar F.M. Rtischev invited pupils at Kievo-Mogilyanskaya Theological Academy, established in 1632, to join the specially formed Saint Andrei Monastery in Moscow in 1649. From these beginnings came the Slavic-Greco-Latin Academy; founded in 1687, this institution became the largest center for religious instruction in Russia.

Saint Dimitriy, Metropolitan of Rostov (1651–1709) and a gifted religious writer, made a substantial contribution to the spiritual treasury of the Russian Church when, in 1684–1705, he compiled and translated the gigantic collection of Saints' Lives, the *Chet'i-Minei*, from Latin and Greek into vernacular Russian. Always combating schismatics within the Church, Dimitriy succeeded in creating models of didactic literature. Perhaps the most important innovators in religious instruction were the Ukrainian theologian Pytor Mogila (d. 1647), the Metropolitan of Kiev, Epifaniy Slavinetsky (d.

1675), and Simeon of Polotsk (1629–80), learned writers of expressive spiritual verse, and Palladiy Pogovsky (d. 1703), the first Russian to achieve a doctorate in philosophy.

In the 17th century, Russian religious culture began to take more account of the progress being made in secular art. Thus, the art of such icon painters as the Muscovites Simon Ushakov (1626–86), Ivan Maksimov (d. 1689), and Vasiliy Poznansky (1655–1710), who, among others, executed paintings in the Kremlin Armory, gradually show evidence of an awareness of Western Europe's realist art. This "discovery of the flesh" would do much to enrich the expressive possibilities of Russia's traditional "spiritual art." Also important, however, was the fruitful development of early Russian representationalism, especially that of the Kholmogory-Ustyug school, headed by Semyon Spiridonov (1642–95); the Kostroma school, with its outstanding master Guriy Nikitin (c. 1630–91); the Yaroslavl and Tikhvin schools of miniature icon-painting; and, finally, the 18th-century Palekh and Mster schools.

From Poland came musical innovation with the appearance of *partesny*, or "harmonic" singing, which replaced Russia's traditional *troestrochnyi*, or "three-voiced" unison system. The Ukrainian composer N.P. Diletsky (1630–90) and Ioannikiy Korenev (17th century), one of the "Church Singers of the Imperial Court," not only founded the new school but also wrote Russia's first treatises on music theory, inspiring the work of such later 17th- and 18-century composers as Vasiliy Titov, Nikolai Kalashnikov, Fyodor Redrikov, and Nikolai Bavykin. This movement developed alongside that of the folk tradition, whose main theoretician was Aleksandr Mezenets. In his *Azbuka* ("ABC") of 1668 Mezenets summarized the century-old experience of Russian sacred music, consolidated the ancient notation system, and established the so-called *znamennyi* notation, which was applied to the monastic tradition of Russian Orthodoxy and is used to this day, albeit in a modified five-line system "with square notes" (1772).

The most significant changes of all occurred in church architecture. Ukrainian and Belorussian masters brought a new architectural style to Russia. Called "Moscow Baroque," the style influenced mainly the central regions of the country. With its checkered red-and-white "brick pattern," similar to East Slavic folk decoration, Moscow Baroque incorporated many elements of the European Baroque. The most illustrious examples are the Church of the "Protecting Veil" at Fili (1693), the Church of the Savior in the village of Ubora (1684–89), the Church of the Dormition on Pokrovka, and the Church of the Icon of the Mother of God at Dubrovitsy (1690–1704). At the beginning of the 18th century Russian Orthodoxy entered a new stage of its history. Peter the Great, the first Russian Emperor (1672–1725), undertook to effect a radical transformation in every aspect of the nation's life. Inspired by the ideas of Western rationalism, the Tsar reformed the Church's administration in 1721, by replacing the Patriarchate with the Spiritual Collegium, then later with the Holy Orthodox Synod. The chief promoter of the new political ideas was Feofan Prokopovich (1681–1736), Bishop of Novgorod, Rector of Kievo-Mogilyanskaya Theological Academy, and author of the Spiritual Regulations, which laid the foundations for the religious reforms of the Petrine era. Opposition, albeit unsuccessful, came from Stefan Yavorskiy (1658–1722), a prominent writer and theologian who became Yoeum Tenens of the Patriarchal See. Joining him in reaction was Feofilact Lopatinsky (1680–1741), Archbishop of Tver, Vice-President of the Holy Synod, and a broadly educated religious figure who in 1721 published Metropolitan Stefan Yavorskiy's most influential essay: "The Rock of Faith." The era of "Enlightened Absolutism" endured in Russia for more than a century, substantially changing the centuries-old relationship between Church and State. Political and economic life, education, and culture were all increasingly secularized, a process wherein the state acquired a large number of Church lands. These changes, however, had the providential effect of deepening the vastly important spiritual growth of the Church. From the 10th century to the 13th, the Church had carried the light of Christian faith to the East Slavic nations, while in the 14th and 15th centuries, it had helped the Russian people regain their spiritual, national, and political independence. Then, in the 16th and 17th centuries, the Church promoted the country's cultural, political, and economic development. Finally, in the 18th and 19th centuries, Orthodoxy found itself undertaking the subtle task of discovering within its mission of salvation the means to untangle the relationship between God and Man.

As if looking at the historical situation in reverse, I.V. Kireyevsky (1806–58), one of the most creative religious thinkers of the 19th century, called upon his colleagues in 1855 to apply their energies "so that the Russian Orthodox spirit, the spirit of true Christian faith, would be embodied in Russian social and family life." From the start of the Synodal period, which lasted two centuries, the Church directed all its healing or charismatic responsibility toward this very goal, but not in a way to hinder the natural-historical process and independent social development of the nation. From decade to decade the Church expanded its creative activities, opening shelters and orphanages, operating hospitals for the sick, and collecting donations to feed the hungry and fight disease. To the farthest reaches of the sparsely populated and still poor country, all the way to Alaska and California, the village church functioned not only as a mystical symbol of "Heaven on earth," but also as a house of joyful tears and mournful sighs, a refuge from every despair, and, most importantly, an elementary school. The sincere (though often not very well educated) parish priest became a real father to his parishioners, sometimes their only teacher, and frequently their only doctor. Thousands of monasteries imperceptibly bound together the "wretched" yet "bountiful" Rus. On fasts and feast days endless lines of pilgrims would wind their way toward the holy places, seeking inner comfort and spiritual joy. It was here, removed from earthly care, that the nation would attend its endless wounds and join in the peace of "the Holy Life."

Through love, through kindness, and through preaching, the Orthodox Church again and again turned back various forms of deviation. The greatest of all the dangers arose from eschatological remnants among the schismatics. Openly proclaiming Peter and his followers to be "antichrists," a few of the schismatics went so far as to implore the faithful to "enter into the life of eternal wandering," to leave the sinful "Tsardom of Babylon," and find the mythical "Tsardom of Opon," situated somewhere in the Far East, "on the border of earth and sky." Although dating from the second half of the 18th century, such folk legends are closely related to the 13th–15th-century Russian prophetic tale of the mysterious holy city of Kitezh (*Kitezh-grad*). This city, protected by the Blessed Virgin and concealed from the Tatar cavalry, lies at the bottom of the Lake of Svetloiar, somewhere in the Volga region. Invisible to the eye of the sinful, the city and churches can be entered only by the chosen few, the "pure of heart," who never return to common reality. The fable constitutes a poetic representation of the schismatic's concept of the "wandering Church," but it also illustrates how the deep Orthodox faith in Christ is preserved in the recesses of the folk spirit. The tale of Kitezh, along with other contemporary legends, comes down to us in one of the more sublime creations of Russian religious folk culture. The festive and

comforting bells ring through the ages, calling the nation to a "holy land" of Orthodox churches and monasteries. There, those who discover the "Holy City" and the "Joys of Eternity" also find the Kingdom of God that "is in us all" (Luke 17:21).

An anonymous essay written at the end of the 19th century, called "The Open Tales of a Wanderer to His Spiritual Son," reveals the mystical nature of Orthodox people. Not only did the ancient Hesychast practice of the continuous Jesus Prayer survive in the Reasonable Prayer of the monks and elders, but it even flourished among many of the laity, there assimilated into the genuinely ascetic life of the Russian faithful, a life concealed from the eyes of the nonbeliever. The search "for the soul" through reasonable prayer, striving in all things to approach the very "heart" of life in its incomprehensible depths, ultimately seeking to elevate and transform sinful human reason through grace—this is the hidden side of Russian Orthodox spirituality, an aspect greatly misunderstood by the educated classes in both Russia and the West during the "Age of Enlightenment" and thereafter.

The leading religious writers of the 18th century, such as the Saint Tikhon of Zadonsk (1724–82) and Paisiy Velichkovsky (1722–94), took it as their lofty pastoral duty to encourage the spiritual enlightenment of the clergy, the monasteries, and the faithful, to preserve and nourish inner piety, and to strengthen the foundations of family, social, and political life. Through their efforts, and those of a number of famous and anonymous hermits of the 18th and 19th centuries, such as the Elder Saint Mefodiy (in Schema Mark) of Sarov (1732–1817), Russian soil was prepared for the grand spiritual activity of succeeding generations.

Russian religious culture in the 18th century, which grew from a variety of sources, was intrinsically whole, yet endured many changes. It was as if the entire land had broken down into fractional "cults" and secular parts. The language reforms sponsored by Peter I left the thousand-year tradition of Church Slavonic for liturgical purposes only. Meanwhile, a new Russian literature was forming in the late 18th century, a literature that would free itself from automatic reliance upon the West, but one that would attain cultural independence only at the end of the century. A significant contribution to this end came in the work of the noted scientist and poet M.V. Lomonosov (1711–65). Born a peasant in Arkhangelsk, a multifaceted and gifted individual, Lemonosov acquired European notoriety through his work in natural science, but in Russia he came to be regarded as a great national poet, one of the founding fathers of the modern Russian language and its literature. His "Reflections on the Greatness of God," a deeply penetrating verse work, stands in striking contrast to the doggerel of the late 17th century and the timid efforts of poets in the post-Petrine era. Lemonosov believed in the symbiotic relationship between the new Russian literary language and the ancient Church Slavonic tradition, making a special case for the relationship in the essay entitled "On the Use of Church Writings in the Russian Language" (1757). It did not take long for his efforts to bear fruit. G.R. Derzhavin's ode "God" became one of the first poetic manifestations of the new Russian literature to receive critical acclaim, as well as translation into many European languages and Japanese. Apart from the historian M.M. Shcherbatov (1733–90) and encyclopedist A.T. Boltov (1738–1833), the only secular writer of the period to return to the almost forgotten religious literary tradition was N.M. Karamzin (1766–1826), who wrote his multivolume *History of the Russian State* in the style of a devout Christian and a true master of words. The brilliant thinker, poet, and writer G.S. Skovoroda, who traveled throughout the Ukrainian lands, provides a shining example of the new era of Russian religious culture. And

further literary achievement can be found in the sermons of Platon (Levshin), Metropolitan of Moscow (1737–1812), an outstanding Church writer and orator.

Eighteenth-century Russian ecclesiastic and religious culture realized its most notable achievements in art, architecture, and music. The trend of the age was towards classicism, which entered the mainstream of Russian academic art through the works of such secular masters as A.P. Antropov, A.P. Losenko, G.I. Kozlov, and A.E. Egorov. Then, when it came time to execute the icons and frescoes for the three most important churches built during the 19th century (St. Petersburg's Cathedral of the Kazan Icon of the Mother of God [1801–11], designed by Voronikhin, and Saint Isaakiy Cathedral [1818–58], built from plans by A.A. Monferran; Moscow's Church of the Savior [1818–83], by the architect K.A. Ton), the commissions went to the leading masters whose training had been academic: G.I. Ugriumov, V.K. Shebuev, F.A. Bruni, K.P. Briullov, P.V. Basin, P.M. Shamshin, S.A. Zhivago, F.S. Zavyalov, and N.A. Maikov. But despite this tradition—a two-century adherence to Greco-Roman and Western artistic motifs—Russian 19th-century religious art returned to the nation's own ancient traditions, which had never ceased to nourish monastic icon painting. Indeed, this art had been brought to brilliant realization by the spiritual asceticism of the masters and all the brethren.

In both St. Petersburg and Moscow, churches constructed in the "Elizabethan Baroque" style (so called for the Empress Elizabeth [r. 1741–62]) incorporated classical motifs and enjoyed a certain fame. The craftsmanship of A.D. Zakharov, I.E. Starov, S.I. Chevakinsky, D.V. Ukhtomsky, V.I. Bazhenov, and M.F. Kazakov made significant contributions to the exterior design of Russian churches and monasteries. Traditional motifs survived only in provincial centers and in the magnificent wooden folk architecture of northern

Russia and Siberia. But the search for a national style of Russian church architecture began with the work of V.I. Bazhenov (1737–99) and continued through the 19th century.

The quest for national form proved more successful in the field of music, where a rich and universally revered folk tradition of choral church singing remained very much alive, although somewhat diminished at the start of the 18th century, owing to a lack of state support. The second half of the century introduced "part" singing, which successfully rivaled the Italian "concert" style introduced from abroad. But Russian church music assumed a national character in the artistry of M.S. Berezovskiy (1745–77), D.S. Bortnyansky (1751–1825), and A.L. Vedel (1767–1806).

Captions

7 Most of the faithful wait until the end of the service for the Patriarch to leave the church. Then as they thank His Holiness once more for his prayers and for the liturgy, they receive a further blessing.

8 The prayer at the Holy Gate of the iconostasis before the beginning of the liturgy.

9 The blessing of the Easter offering— Easter cake (*kulich*), Easter cheese (*paskha*), and painted eggs—on Holy Saturday in the Church of the Assumption at the Trinity–Saint Sergiy Lavra in Zagorsk.

10–13 The Russian Orthodox Church knows no happier event, nor any greater feast, than Easter, the Resurrection of Christ. On the last day of the long Lenten fast, in the evening before Easter Sunday, the faithful carry their Easter offerings into the church to have them blessed. They have decorated the gifts in a springlike fashion, albeit with paper, rather than real, flowers due to the lingering cold of winter. Thousands of candles announce the new light and fill the chilly churches with a gentle, crackling sound. The Easter offerings, symbolic of the beginning of new life and the promise of Heavenly bliss, are then taken home and consumed among friends.

14 Here, at the refectory of the Trinity–Saint Sergiy Lavra, the cross is carried in solemn procession after matins throughout Holy Week.

15 In memory of the Last Supper, when Christ broke bread with his Disciples, a large *prosfora* ("sacrificial bread") is baked with the seal of the cross IC XC NIKA ("Jesus Christ is victorious") imprinted on it. Called by its Greek name, *Artos*, the bread is always blessed on the first day of Easter, and during Easter Week it remains on the altar or on one of the icon stands. Because it symbolizes the Paschal Lamb as well as the bread of life, the *Artos* is always carried at the head of the Easter Week processions.

16 Archimandrite Bulogios, the steward of Trinity–Saint Sergiy Lavra and a professor at the Moscow Theological Academy, sprinkles holy water on brethren and faithful during the Easter procession.

17 For the Russian Church, Easter is a cosmic event that embraces all people and all things. Thus, Christ's descent into Hell for the redemption of his forefathers—which the Orthodox Church commemorates on Holy Saturday—constitutes the basic typology of the Resurrection itself. The icon here shows Christ leading the ancestors by the hand out of Hell, while breaking down its gate with his feet. The corresponding passage in the Easter *troparion* reads: "Having conquered death, Christ is risen from the dead and brings new life to those who rest in their graves."

10

11

12

13

17

The Patriotic War of 1812, fought against the Napoleonic invasion, shook all of Russian society. "Enlightened" French soldiers desecrated such national shrines as the Cathedrals of the Moscow Kremlin, but these and other heinous acts served only to rally the entire nation to a sacred struggle for the liberation of the homeland. Blessing and inspiring the Russians' just cause, the Orthodox Church incited and spiritually fortified the patriotic feelings of the nation. It also rendered material assistance, organized help for the wounded, for invalids, for the families of those killed in action, collected donations, and provided financial aid to the ravaged and hungry throughout the country.

In the 19th century Russia continued to lead a diplomatic and political struggle, begun in the 16th century, for the complete liberation of Orthodox nations, whatever the fetters that still bound them. Eventually, in the 18th and 19th centuries, the noble efforts of Orthodox believers resulted in a series of wars with Turkey. This brought tormented Georgia under the protection of Russia in 1801, and almost thirty years later Greece and Rumania won their decisive independence from Turkey after the Russo-Turkish War of 1828–29. In the war of 1878–79, the Russian Army heroically brought freedom to Bulgaria and Serbia, which, like the other Balkan countries, had been under the Turkish yoke for centuries.

The Church's peaceful missionary activity, so true to the spirit of Orthodoxy, continued to be an integral part of the Russian character, even in the darkest of times. During this period, the Church brought the beneficent light of Christian faith to many countries and nationalities in both Asia and America. At the end of the 18th century, a monk from the Valaam Monastery, Saint Yerman of Alaska, tirelessly preached in and brought religious instruction to the Kamchatka Peninsula, the Aleutian Islands, and the shores of Alaska. He was canonized by the Autocephalous Orthodox Church of America in 1970. The first Orthodox Bishop on the North American continent, Blessed Innokentiy (Veniaminov) of Siberia (1840), settled on the island of Unalashka and made it the center of Russian missionary activity in the Aleutians, where he and his clergy preached in local languages, set down their alphabets, and translated many sacred writings. In the 19th century, Orthodox spiritual missions were either established or expanded in Siberia, Central Asia, the Far East, China and Korea, the Caucasus, and the Volga area. Thanks to the missionary Urmia, thousands of Assyrian and Nestorian Christians adopted Orthodoxy. In 1847 the Russian Spiritual Mission in Jerusalem came into being, an event that successfully strengthened fraternal ties between the Jerusalem and Russian Orthodox Churches. Since then, the flow of Russian pilgrims to the Holy Land has never let up. Syria and Palestine, once freed from Turkish domination, received important assistance in their renewal of Orthodoxy through the Orthodox Palestine Society, organized in 1882, which maintained more than a hundred schools and for decades carried out a great deal of archaeological and historical investigation in Jerusalem and outlying areas. In 1870, Saint Nikolai of Japan (1836–1912), Equal of the Apostles and canonized by the Russian Orthodox Church in 1970, founded the Russian Spiritual Mission in Japan. Originally a peasant from Smolensk, this holy man completely mastered the Japanese language and succeeded in immersing himself in the spiritual life of the people. In the end he overcame their initial hostility and won tens of thousands of hearts for Christ. Nikolai's translations of the Gospels and other liturgical works into Japanese were even accepted by the missions of the Western Churches in Japan. Not only did the young Japanese Church stand firm during the difficult days of the Russo-Japanese War of 1904–05, but through the wise leadership of their archpastor, Saint Nikolai, the Church vastly increased its spiritual treasures. As an enlightener and a peace-maker, Saint Nikolai was revered by the population with the same devotion as that accorded the Emperor. He even managed to draw the Japanese people closer to an understanding of the spiritual foundations of Russian culture, inspiring their love and steadfast interest in its highest forms.

These achievements would not have been possible without the continuing inner development of the Church in Russia itself. A unified system of religious instruction and education brought the entire believing nation closer to the treasures of the Orthodox spiritual experience. The large theological schools and centers of religious instruction were the Moscow, St. Petersburg, Kiev, and Kazan Theological Academies, but anyone who thirsted for knowledge could receive instruction and spiritual nourishment from the schools, seminaries, and parochial elementary schools found in every diocese. Leading theologians and religious figures of the first half of the 19th century were Metropolitan Filaret (Drozdov; 1785–1867) of Moscow, Metropolitan Evgeniy (Bolkhovitinov; 1767–1837) of Kiev and Archibishop Filaret (Gumilevskii; 1805–66) of Chernigov. They succeeded in combining asceticism, comprehensive education, and complete mastery of the methods of historical-philosophical analysis with ecclesiastical and social activity. To achieve all its purposes, the Russian Orthodox Church required an enlightened pastoral service.

In a relatively short time, the theological academies and the theological faculties of the universities educated an entire galaxy of noted theologians, historians, and philosophers, philologists and linguists, many highly respected in scholarly circles. With the active support of Moscow Metropolitan Filaret, the historians Archpriest A.V. Gorsky and K.I. Nevostruev

concluded the monumental work of the Russian Bible Society (established in 1813) when their complete scholarly translation of the Bible, the first thing of its kind in Russia, appeared in 1876. Meanwhile, leading academic scholars, such as Metropolitan Makariy (Bulgakov) of Moscow, I.V. Cheltsov, A.P. Lebedev, A.P. Spassky, E.E. Golubinsky, N.N. Glubokovsky, and V.V. Bolotov, conducted research in a number of areas in theology, Church history, and archaeology. Toward the middle of the 19th century, the compatability of the Christian faith, and its development, with scientific endeavor became a major theme of such religious philosophers as Professors P.D. Yurkevich, F.F. Sidonsky, and O.M. Novitsky, as well as of Archimandrite Gavriil (Voskresensky), who wrote the first history (in six volumes) of secular philosophy in Russia (1837–40), and encyclopedist S.S. Gogotsky, author of the four-volume *Philosophical Lexicon* (1857–73). At the beginning of the 20th century, a thorough study of the Orthodox liturgy was carried out by academic theologians and professors I.D. Mansvetov, A.P. Golubtsov, N.V. Pokrovsky, A.A. Dmitrievsky, N.F. Krasnoseltsev, and M.N. Skaballanovich.

These undeniable achievements resulted from the inconspicuous, yet close and beneficial, relations between academic scholarship, spiritual experience of the Russian Orthodox Church, and its great zealots in the 19th century. One of the latter was Saint Serafim of Sarov (1759–1833), an inextinguishable flame of the Russian land, a Patron Saint of the nation, and its prayerful representative before God. This miracle-worker is often compared to Catholicism's Saint Francis of Assisi, despite the different cultural traditions they represent. Saint Serafim of Sarov dedicated his life to God, and now, as he did in his own time, this holy man represents the age-old religious experience of the Russian Orthodox Church and all of Eastern Orthodoxy. There is hardly a Russian soul that would not be moved by these blessed words, spoken with each of us in mind: "My joy, find the Holy Spirit, that thousands of souls may be saved around you." Saint Serafim was himself a living witness to the divine, eternal power within the sincere and believing heart. So that he might be heard by the entire nation, he abandoned the world at the end of the 18th century for the silence of the Sarov forests near Arzamas. To the faint of heart, to the poor in spirit, he said: "God is like a fire that warms the heart and the belly." Both simple illiterates and the more educated of subsequent generations recall his uniquely Russian commandment to "stand with your mind in your heart," to warm knowledge with "the warmth of the heart," so that we may arrive at a peaceful order and "complete unity." Eventually the Saint's rustic cell grew into a major pilgrimage center: the Diveyev Monastery of Saint Serafim and Sarov Hermitage.

At the same time, other centers of Orthodox culture grew and multiplied. Among the most important of these was the Optyna Hermitage on the border of the Kaluga Province outside the city of Kozelsk. According to tradition, the hermitage came into being sometime during the 14th century, but did not flourish until the late 18th and early 19th centuries. By the 1850s the modest cloister had been transformed into a palladium of Russian spirituality. To attain wisdom and spiritual comfort, some of the geniuses of Russian literature and philosophy would gather about the elders of the Optyna Hermitage. There, at one time or another could be found the poet V.A. Zhukovsky, the Slavophile brothers I.V. and P.V. Kireyevsky, A.S. Khomiakov, I.S. Aksakov, Iu. F. Samarin, the writers Gogol and Dostoyevsky, the philosophers Leontiev and Rozanov, and many, many others. The elders of the monastery— hieroschema monks Feofan (d.1819), Lev (1768–1841), Makariy (d. 1860); Fathers Ambrosiy (Grenkov; 1812–93), Iosif (1837–1911), Varsonofiy (d. 1912), Anastasiy (d. 1922), and Nectariy (d.

1923)—may in all truth be called major exponents of the Russian literary and philosophical culture of the 19th and early 20th centuries. Then, there was Vyshenskaya Wilderness, hidden in the forests of the Penza region. It became a refuge for Bishop Feofan the Recluse (Govorov; 1815–94), a leading religious teacher of the late 19th century, who compiled the five-volume work *Loving Kindness* (*Dobrotolyubie*), a new translation of selected works of the holy fathers of Eastern Orthodoxy. Bishop Ignatiy (Bryanchaninov; 1807–67) was another of the period's brilliant theologians and gifted religious writers.

In the 19th century the spiritual leadership of the Russian Orthodox Church provided a firm support for the moral enrichment of Russia. The nation's artists returned to their religious heritage, and culture appeared as an intrinsically whole rather than a fragmented and isolated phenomenon, all of which determined the most important directions in the development of painting, music, and architecture. In church architecture of the 1830s and 1840s, the classical and imperial styles would yield to the so-called Byzantine style, which can be seen most graphically in the work of V.P. Stasov and K.A. Ton, who designed that famous monument to the heroes of the Patriotic War of 1812, the Cathedral of Christ the Savior in Moscow (1832–83). It is also evident in the illustrious complex of buildings at Valaam Monastery planned by M.D. Bykovsky and A.M. Gornostaev. In the second half of the century Russian architects finally overcame the influence of the traditional academic school represented by R.I. Kuzminin and D.I. Grimm, and the style that emerged reflects the essential features of late Byzantine and early Russian architecture applied to the "canon" of joyous, "flowering" Beauty, but realized with contemporary construction techniques. The resulting peculiarities, present in churches throughout the country, could correctly be described as constituting a uniquely "Russian" style.

Pictorial art had lost its living ties to traditional Russian icon painting, and religious themes could scarcely be found outside the work of such masters as I.N. Kramskoi, G.I. Semiradsky, N.N. Ghe, and P.A. Svedomsky. Only the genius A.I. Ivanov may be truly called a leading Russian religious painter of the 19th century.

In the realm of religious music, however, a rich heritage of Russian national and Western European traditions had existed and developed for a hundred years, not only in church-related folk culture but within the Orthodox liturgical canon as well. The church music of A.F. Lvov, M.I. Glinka, the religious choral music of A.S. Arensky, the work of G.A. Lomakin, P.M. Vorotnikov, N.I. Bakhmetev, and G.F. Lvovsky, and the arrangements of N.M. Potulov are performed in religious communities to this day. The numerous religious works of P.I. Tchaikovsky enlarged upon the compositions of A.T. Grechaninov, S.V. Panchenko, E.S. Azeyev, and G.F. Lvovsky with their closer proximity to the strict Russian Church style. But the most important religious composer was, of course, A.D. Kastalsky (1856–1926), who combined European musical forms with ancient ecclesiastical traditions and Russia'a national artistic heritage. He even established an entire school of talented followers, such as P.G. Chesnokov, A.A. Arkhangelsky, and Archpriest Dimitriy Allemanov.

In the course of the 19th century, Russian religious culture made a complete return to its spiritual and national roots. Only an outsider would have failed to perceive the depths of these creative sources. They were able to feed the great sea of Russian culture, which by the beginning of the 20th century had succeeded in reaching out to all corners of the globe.

As Russia entered our present century it also approached the time of its most difficult trials.

During the Russo-Japanese War of 1904–05 and then World War I, the Church used all its power to collect funds for the benefit of the victims of war and social disorder, rendering massive material and spiritual aid to the hungry, the wounded, orphans and widows, the old and the invalid.

The Church felt the need to raise the question of restoring the Patriarchate. On the initiative of Metropolitan Antoniy (Vadkovsky) and Archbishop Sergiy (Stragorodsky), a pre-council committee (1906–07), made up of representatives of the clergy and laity, came into being. This was in anticipation of an all-Russian Local Council that would meet to restore the Patriarchate, but, owing to interruptions caused by war, the preparations dragged on for ten years. Finally, on October 28 (November 10), 1917, the council made its historic decision to restore the Patriarchate, and on November 5 (18) Moscow Metropolitan Tikhon (Belavin; 1865–1925) was elected as the new Patriarch of Moscow and All Russia. He would head the Church along with the Synod and the High Church Council.

Concurrently with revolutionary modifications in Russia's social and political structure, important changes occurred in the internal organization of the Russian Orthodox Church. Church and State had to establish mutual relations, thanks to an unusually complex set of historical conditions, which had directed the nation into a completely new mode of development.

Until that time, the age-old spiritual heritage of the Russian Orthodox Church had been instilled in the communal experience of its flock. Not impoverished, but fulfilled, the Church was prepared to brave the cleansing tribulations that were to come. At the beginning of this century, many rediscovered the treasury of Russian spiritual culture. Veneration of the holy relics of the Lord's numerous saints, the tireless pastoral activity of His priests, the prayerful and blessed activity of the Church servants, the monks, and the nuns in many churches and monasteries, the continuous intercession of the Heavenly Church, and the unnoticed deeds of untold numbers of anonymous righteous men— all supplied the believing nation with a great spiritual strength. This was the time when, in the quiet of Athos, the schemamonk Siluan (Antonov; 1866–1938) was offering up his prayers for the entire world. The light from this lantern of Orthodox piety did not become evident to the faithful until years after the saintly man's passing. But many other zealots have also stood firm before God, in their "faith, hope, and love" promoting prayer for the entire world.

Throughout the ages, the Western world has seen Russia as a "sleeping giant" and reproached it for what appeared to be stagnation and ignorance. But in its heart, Russia could simply not accept the transient values so easily absorbed by far-away cultures, preferring instead to zealously guard its own untarnished shrines. And the lack of any great interest in a "cultural dialogue" can be explained by Orthodoxy's ascetic practice of "concealing one's spiritual gifts." Non-Orthodox cultures would accept the authentic greatness of Orthodoxy only through its countless mediators, now universally recognized as representatives of late 19th- and early-20th-century Russia's religious intelligentsia. The direct predecessors of those Orthodox intellectuals were the *Liubomudry*, or "Lovers of Wisdom," who flourished in the 1820s and 1830s, the mid-19th-century Slavophiles, and such religious thinkers as the ideologists of the late-19th-century *Pochvennichestvo* ("Men of the Soil") movement. Among the latter appeared A.A. Grigoriev, N.N. Strakhov, and such subsequent Slavophiles as N. Ia. Danilevsky and K.N. Leontiev, who sought an authentic national basis for spirituality, deeming it essential to *sobornost* ("communality") and to the sure presence of religious values in the consciousness and in the entire life of the individual.

The illustrious group of writers, artists, and thinkers of Russia's "Silver Age" formed a new cultural stratum in the country. Through St. Petersburg's "Religious Philosophical Meetings" of 1901–03, as well as through many other literary and artistic salons and circles of both Russian capitals, an entire generation of intelligentsia became familiar with the great spiritual values of Orthodoxy, even when these were well hidden in the depths of religious and national life. The work of the poet V.S. Solovyev (1853–1900), a leading philosopher and theologian, greatly influenced the religious culture of 20th-century Russia. The concept of the indivisibility of truth, beauty, and goodness, so traditional in Russian religious thought, is reflected in his ideas of the "total unity of reality," which can be perceived only as "indivisible knowledge." Among the followers of Solovyev were the writers, poets, and artists of the Symbolist school, such as philosophers and theologians S.N. and E.H. Trubetskoi, the priest S.N. Bulgakov, N.A. Berdyaev, and a large group of professors from the Orthodox Theological Institute in Paris, founded in 1924. Perhaps the most original thinkers were N.F. Fedorov, who established the Russian tradition of "Christian cosmism"; V.V. Rozanov, the perceptive investigator of the deep layers of religious consciousness; and V.I. Nesmelov, famous for his work in the field of Orthodox anthropology.

An important role in the development of modern Russia's theological thought was played by Father Pavel Florenskiy (1882–1943), whose research led him to discover the *entelelkhiia* (*entelecheia* in Greek)—that is, the end-cause of evolution, its various material processes, and their ultimate formation within the one "cosmic" Church of the universe transformed by God. N.O. Lossky (1870–1965), noted philosopher and since 1947, professor at the Russian Academy in New York, later developed some of Solovyev's ideas in an all-inclusive system of "integral intuitivism." Also well known in the Russian Orthodox world is the remarkable research in the history of Russian religious culture carried out by G.P. Fedotov, who in 1930 founded the League of Orthodox Culture in Paris, the Archpriest G.V. Florovsky, L.P. Karsavin, and many others. Unfortunately, their work all too often reveals an unyielding hostility to the Russian Orthodox Church and the Soviet government as well as a bitter resistence to the changes that have occurred since the Revolution of 1917.

Sermons are an inseparable part of the liturgical life. From the beginning of the 20th century, such notable works as the essays of Father Aleksiy Mechev, Bishop of Luka (Voino-yasenetsky), and other famous or anonymous writers have greatly influenced the life of the Church.

The religious fiction of 20th-century Russia continued the traditions of A.S. Pushkin, I.S. Nikitin, F.I. Tyutchev, N.S. Leskov, Gogol, and F.M. Dostoyevsky and produced a number of talented writers, poets, and journalists. The heated novels of I.S. Schmelev, the sensitive and almost contemplative "musical" writings of B.K. Zaitsev, the inimitable "Byzantine," "plaited words" of A.M. Remizov, S.N. Kylchkov, and N.A. Klyuev, the philosophical lyrics of V.I. Ivanov and G.V. Ivanov, and the verse and plays of Sr. Maria (E. Iu. Kuzmina-Karavaeva), who perished heroically in a Nazi concentration camp in 1945, constitute only a few of the more important works to be achieved in this period. But those who wrote from abroad revealed in their writing the bitter despair and nostalgic sentimentality of Russian emigration.

In the architecture and the pictorial arts of 20th-century Russia the intense search of the previous decades finally caught up with Church traditions, thanks to the efforts of the restorers and art historians, who brought Russian painting and architecture back to life. The oldest landmarks of

Russian religious art and architecture began to be studied in the 1830s and 1840s, a phase that was followed by a second one lasting from the 1860s through the 1880s. Then, after the turn of the 20th century came the stunning discoveries of early Russian icon painting, which generated a whole new interest. Once the Society for the Preservation of Ancient Monuments had been formed, it began sponsoring a number of specialized journals, such as *Sofia* (1914), as well as the first exhibitions of old icons (1911). This latent cultural movement quickly gained the forefront in Russian artistic life. When it came to architecture, the work of V.M. Vasnetsov in the 1880s and 1890s, like the notable creations of A.V. Shchusev in the early 20th century, had an indelible impact on the styles of V.A. Pokrovsky, A.E. Bondarenko, and S.S. Krichinsky, the latter remembered for his Cathedral of the Feodorovskaya Icon of the Mother of God at Tsarskoe Selo (1914). In marked contrast to the work of V.M. Vasnetsov, V.D. Polenov, and M.A. Vrubel, which departed significantly from Church canon, appeared the first pictures of K.S. Petrov-Vodkin, who took inspiration from early Russian icon painting, and the graphics of V.A. Favorsky and V. Ia. Bilibin, who drew upon early Russian manuscript illustrations. In 1914 V.I. Surikov in his *Annunciation* returned to religious themes, as had M.V. Nesterov in his marvelous canvases of a slightly earlier date and the first works of D.S. Stelletsky, so well known for the commission he undertook at the Podvorye of Saint Sergiy in Paris. Then, there is the special artistic merit of the folk art produced by the masters of Palekh, Mstera, and Kholui.

From the beginning of the 20th century, ecclesiastical music developed along the same lines as secular symphonic compositions, which can be seen in the choral cantatas of S.I. Taneyev. In 1915 S.V. Rachmaninov produced his famous *Vespers,* considered one of the landmarks of

20th-century a capella music, and in 1917 A.D. Kastalskiy wrote and performed his *Prayer for Those Perished During the War*. A spiritual colleague of the latter was N.N. Cherepnin. Other interesting compositions came from the pen of V.A. Bogadurov, V.I. Rebikov, the fine lyricist M.M. Ippolitov-Ivanov, and even the modernist I.F. Stravinskiy. The Western Christian world eventually became familiar with early and contemporary Russian liturgical music through the incomparable performances of the illustrious choral ensemble of N.P. Afonsky, the Patorzhinsky Quartet, and numerous Cossack choirs, especially the Russian symphonic choir of Kibalchich, formed in New York in 1924. The heightened spirituality, the fascinating sense of melody, the enormous inner dynamism evinced by the Russian people through their Orthodox Church music have the power to capture the heart of even the most jaded listener. Moreover, the major works of Russian folk and religious culture, ranging from the 11th to the 20th century, served to establish the first deep contacts of the Russian Orthodox Church with Western Christianity, thereby making possible a greater breadth in both cultural exchange and theological dialogue.

Over the centuries, the Russian Orthodox Church has survived the abominable Tatar Yoke, the *oprichnina* of Ivan the Terrible, the religious schisms of the 17th century, the peasant uprisings of later times, the despotic power of Peter I, and an almost uninterrupted series of wars. Yet, the very harshness of these tribulations has served to deepen the already profound spiritual experience of the Russian nation and to confirm its readiness to confess the Orthodox faith in the face of every external circumstance. The interrelationship between Russian Orthodoxy and the Russian State has always been determined by the national and religious unity of the Church and the people, who share a common historical fate.

Transcending all else, Primates of the Orthodox Church concern themselves with preaching the Gospel, whatever the conditions, and with calling for moral purification and the preservation within society of the spirit of Evangelical peace, love, and mercy.

The overthrow of the Russian monarchy and the establishment of the Soviet political system were a stormy manifestation of the Russian people's age-old desire for a just world order. At the same time the Synodal period of Russian Church history came to an end. On September 1, 1917, the Local Council of the Russian Orthodox Church passed a resolution announcing the "nonparticipation of the Russian Orthodox Church in the struggle of the political parties." The purpose of the resolution was not to prevent the Church's members from participating in the events then unfolding in Russian national life, but rather to help them adjust to the situation wisely. Then, on January 23, 1918, the Soviet authorities issued a decree. Entitled "On the Separation of the Church from the State, and Schools from the Church," it defined the new legal status of the Russian Orthodox Church. Meanwhile, Article 124 of the 1936 Constitution provided legislative confirmation for the freedom to confess the faith in the U.S.S.R. And in the new Constitution of 1977, Article 52 upholds the rights of believers "to practice any religion."

The first years of Soviet rule—the years of devastation, hunger, social anarchy, destruction, and mass death in the countryside—were a time of great sacrifice for the whole of Russia. From the beginning of World War I to the early 1920s the nation lost ten million people. But since its inception, the Church had instilled within the Russian people a readiness to endure suffering and self-sacrifice, all of which gave believers the capacity and the power to withstand terrible trials. Moreover, the Church never ceased to see a higher purpose in those events. Along with the entire nation, the Church's new Primate managed to discover the right path through the thicket of difficulties, doing so with tranquil resolve. In 1919 the Most Holy Patriarch Tikhon insisted that both clergy and laymen exclude politics from Church life. He led a new struggle against schism within the Church, a problem that had become prevalent both inside Russia and beyond its borders. In violation of the commands of Orthodoxy, many clerics fell in with the schismatics, and many among the hierarchy destroyed canonical order by standing in the way of Moscow Patriarchate's efforts to reconcile the Church and the Soviet authorities. Now came the movement for Church "renewal," which led to a number of diverse heresies (the "Living Church," "Self-baptists," among others). The whole experience proved to be a shameless negation of the Gospel and of patristic teaching about the Church, its dogma and national historic traditions. Clearly inspired by an expedient reaction to circumstances, the renewal movement led to appalling losses and inflated religious hostility. But the Most Holy Patriarch Tikhon steadfastly and vigorously shored up the foundations of unity within the Russian Orthodox Church. On the eve of his death in 1925, he instructed his followers "…not sinning against our faith and the Church, not compromising or making concessions in matters of faith, in civil affairs to be honest in relations with Soviet government and to work for the common good…" Thus directed, the Church developed in a way that led to a gradual normalization of relations within the Soviet authorities, which permitted all manner of trouble and divisiveness within the Church to be eventually overcome.

Patriarch Tikhon was succeeded by Sergiy (Stragorodksky; 1867–1944), who served as Metropolitan of Nizhny Novgorod and Loeum-Tenens of the Patriarchal See and since 1943 as Patriarch of Moscow and All Russia. Anxious to end the misunderstandings of the changes within the country, Metropolitan Sergiy, through the Holy Synod, appealed to the sons and daughters of the Church in 1927, calling for loyalty to the Soviet regime: "We want to remain Orthodox, yet at the same time we recognize the Soviet Union as our civic Homeland." Everlasting faith in the foundations of Orthodoxy, love of the Motherland, a fervent sense of national pride, and the national independence of the Russian Church united all those Christians committed to Patriarchal authority. Under the wise leadership of Metropolitan Sergiy, the Church did not lose its spiritual authority, however great its material impoverishment. During the 1920s and 1930s many church goers abstained from traditional religious observance, but without losing their deep, heart-felt ties to the Mother Church, which remained the bearer of the highest moral commandments. A number of parishes ceased to exist, but pure human hearts remained open to God. The ever-living Word continued to be heard in the conscience of the most desperate and faithless.

Like a deadly fire storm, a new World War descended on Russia in 1941. Again the country survived a bitter struggle with the enemy, this time at a cost of more than 20 million lives, more than 1,700 destroyed towns and cities, and tens of thousands of burned and trampled villages. In the very first days of the conflict the Primate of the Russian Orthodox Church rallied the nation's believers: "Not during the time of the Princely Wars, nor under Tatar Yoke, nor during the Time of Troubles, has the Russian Church abandoned its earthly Motherland…." As in earlier centuries, when Saint Sergiy of Radonezh blessed Russian warriors and foretold victory in the coming battle with Mamai, the Tatar Kahn, so did Metropolitan Sergiy bless the nation for the tasks that lay before it, kindling the heart of every believer with faith that triumph over Nazism would be attained. During the years of this horrible war, the sister

Churches also prayed for the victory of the Soviet Army over "the forces of Satan." To aid in this cause the Russian Orthodox Church provided financial support and collected warm clothes throughout the country, as well as gifts for the army, the wounded, for invalids and orphans. In occupied territories, the faithful courageously battled with the enemy and participated in partisan activities. At Orel, the priest-patriots N. Obolensky and T. Orlov died heroically in combat with the fascists. Thousand of believers and clerics and many hierarchs would receive the highest honors in recognition of their heroic patriotism.

The literature of the war years bears witness to Orthodox fervor—deepened by a thousand years of experience—that pervaded the Russian people, their moral stability, and their purity. To understand this spirituality, which the Russian soldier defended, one need only to read the verses of Aleksandr Tvardovsky. In "The Church of Saint Nicholas," a marvelous work written by Alexei Nedogonov during his participation in the battles near Shipka (Bulgaria) in 1944, the poet remarks that, like his ancestors of olden times, "I approached the church with the soldiers of glory, through Stalingrad, through fire and smoke, and with my weapon won the right to kneel before it." As a result of the severe trials brought by the Great Patriotic War, the Russian people found the image of Christ re-created within themselves, and the believing Russian nation gained a more acute understanding of its everlasting ties with the Mother Church.

In September 1943, the Council of Hierarchs of the Russian Orthodox Church elected Metropolitan Sergiy to the Patriarchal See. For millions of believers, the joy of decisive victory and of liberation from fascist oppression coincided with the ineffable spiritual joy of the Easter celebrations in 1944 and 1945. Adherence to the sacred mysteries, warm communal prayers for the Motherland, common grief over the untold losses shared in the Church—through all this Russia renewed itself in united spiritual vigor. The West, to this day, circulates a "Russian legend," which explains the massive self-sacrifice at the front and the indescribable national fortitude of Russia behind the lines in terms of a "lack of concern" for the individual, of "collective irrationality," etc. Here, one should be reminded of words written by the 19th-century poet F.I. Tiutchev: "One cannot understand Russia with the mind; she cannot be measured with a yardstick. Rather she has a special bearing: in Russia one can only believe."

On the eve of his death in 1944 (May 15) Holy Patriarch Sergiy nominated as his successor Aleksiy (Simansky), Metropolitan of Leningrad and Novgorod, now remembered for his heroic pastoral service during the 900-day siege of Leningrad. In February 1945, a National Church Council met to name him as the new Patriarch.

From the moment he was elected, Patriarch Aleksiy (1877–1970) found himself confronted with Church problems of a very serious order. Russia had been burned from north to south by the flames of the most devastating war in all of history. But the nation's utterly selfless, unremitting labor to rebuild the postwar economy was evenly matched by its formidable efforts to meet the needs of the Church. Incinerated monasteries and churches were rebuilt, brought back to life, and filled with attendants, icons, church implements, liturgical vestments, and prayer books. In 1945, the Publications Department of the Moscow Patriarchate came into being, and in 1946 the Department of External Church Relations and other departments of the Moscow Patriarchate. Meanwhile, in 1944, the Theological Courses for Pastors and the Theological Institute had been introduced at Moscow's Novodevich Convent. Models for other seminaries and academies, they were moved in 1948 to the Trinity—Saint Sergiy Lavra in Zagorsk. The spiritual and material well-being of the Russian monasteries and convents became the overriding concern of His Holiness Patriarch Aleksiy. The nation's fervent love of churches and liturgy, especially religious singing, assured a complete renewal of the best traditions of Orthodox Church service.

The hierarchs of the Russian Church spared no effort in overcoming the destructive internal schisms of the late 1920s and 1930s. Energetically and diplomatically, Patriarch Aleksiy brought numerous disenchanted groups closer to the One Russian Orthodox Church. From the very start of his tenure, hierarchs and clerics of the *Obnovlenchestvo* ("renewal") movement were, after public repentance, accepted into communion with the rest of the Church. Also restored were some parishes in Belorussia, Moldavia, and the Ukraine, which had deviated into various schismatic tendencies during the foreign occupation. From 1945 to 1949, adherents of the so-called "Estonian" schism were accepted back, as were Greek-Catholics (Uniates) of the Western Ukraine and Carpathia, who in 1946 renounced the Union of Brest (1596) at their Church Council of Clergy and Laity in Lvov.

The moral and patriotic role played by the Russian Orthodox Church during World War II won the sympathy of many Russian Orthodox Christians living abroad, and this paved the way for the restoration of canonical relations between the Russian Orthodox Church and many of the schismatics abroad. In 1945 the Moscow Patriarchate granted jurisdiction to the clergy and parishes of Western Europe headed by Metropolitan Evlogiy (Georgievsky). Many hierarchs, clerics, and laymen of the "Karlovtsy schism," which, calling itself the "Russian Orthodox Church Abroad," had been located in Western Europe, America, China, Bulgaria, and Yugoslavia, also received jurisdiction from the Moscow Patriarchate. In 1948 the Russian Spiritual Mission in Jerusalem resumed its activities. That

same year the Russian Orthodox Church extended autocephaly to the Polish Orthodox Church and in 1951 to the Czechoslovakian Orthodox Church. In 1970 the Autocephalous Russian Orthodox Church in North America came into being, and the Japanese Orthodox Church gained autonomy. During the war and its immediate aftermath, traditional fraternal ties between the Russian Church and other local Orthodox Churches were restored and strengthened. Simultaneously, the Russian Church began searching for new forms of ecumenical cooperation with non-Orthodox Churches, such as the ancient non-Chalcedonian Eastern Churches of Armenia, Ethiopia, and Coptic Egypt. Under His Holiness Patriarch Aleksiy there was a fruitful rapprochement with Anglicans, as well as with Baptists and Old Catholics. Moreover, meetings began with representatives of the Roman Catholic Church.

It should not be surprising that after the nation's victorious emergence from World War II the Russian Orthodox Church immediately began taking part in the international peace movement. Thus, in 1945 the Church's Local Council came out with a peace-making appeal to all Christians. Then in 1948, at the suggestion of Patriarch Aleksiy, the leaders and representatives of the Autocephalous Orthodox Churches, while meeting to celebrate the Russian Church's five hundred years of independence, delivered an "Address to Christians of All Nations," with the objective of preventing a new world catastrophe. In 1949–50 representatives of the Russian Orthodox Church helped create the World Council of Peace, and over the next few decades Russian Orthodox delegates participated in a series of international forums with other religious leaders devoted to disarmament and the struggle for world peace. The Russian Orthodox Church's constant promotion of the cause of peace in our time constitutes a visible expression of its commitment to the fate of mankind as well as a manifestation of its maternal care for the preservation of the lives of its children.

After the death of Patriarch Aleksiy in April 1970, a Local Council of the Russian Church, the third in the short history of the reestablished Patriarchate, convened in May–June 1971 at the Trinity– Saint Sergiy Lavra and there elected Pimin (Izvekov; b. 1910), Metropolitan of Krutitsy and Kolomna as the fourteenth Patriarch of Moscow and All Russia. One of the main purposes of this council was to revoke the anathema passed by the Council of 1667 against the Old Believers and thus place before the Russian Church's long-divided offspring conditions for restoring Orthodox unity. Next on the agenda came the canonization of Bishop Nikolai of Japan (d. 1912) and Saint Yerman of Alaska (d. 1837). In 1977 Metropolitan Innokentiy (Veniaminov) was also canonized.

The believing Christian now knows that the absence of war has become the most important condition for the continued existence of all mankind, as well as for the complete fulfillment of social, family, and personal life. But he has not necessarily aquired his own, ardently desired inner peace. Following the commandment of the Church Fathers, to perform "constant works of spirituality," the Russian Church must contend with a number of unresolved problems, both old and new, and struggle with evil of every sort. Often this evil is individual; at other times it assumes a social character. Above all else, the Russian Church sees its traditional responsibility as the revelation of the mysteries of Christian faith to all its members for the duration of their earthly lives. The liturgical, prayerful, and sacred ties between the Church and its children and from believer to believer form the basis of Orthodox spiritual and ecclesiastical life. This phenomenon is reflected in the almost complete absence of religious clubs, societies, and special religious groups throughout

Russian history. Relations within the Church itself are sincere, prayerful, and almost inconspicuous, just as the Church is itself "inconspicuous" in contemporary society. In no way does the Church regulate social conditions; instead, it exerts a quiet yet beneficent effect on the foundations of society, summoning all its members to fulfill the everlasting ideals of Orthodoxy. The problem of the "social responsibility of the Church," which worries the contemporary Western world, has been solved by Russian Orthodoxy, not through proselytizing, but rather through quiet, constant sermons among its members. The Church does not create, nor does it try to create, new social institutions to suit the needs of one moment, preferring instead to bless any socially useful activity performed by its members in their jobs, in their acts of mercy, and in their daily lives.

Like the Western Church, Russian Orthodoxy is concerned with the problems of contemporary youth. Even here, rather than encourage a superficial confession of faith, the Church tries to help young people avoid sin, to nourish and strengthen the will to good in those who approach "troubled and burdened." The Church rejoices in the multitude of its children, mourns their losses, and prayerfully cares for the faint of heart and the prodigal; it fortifies the ill, the advanced in years, the lonely, and all who grieve. Slowly but surely, such acts of mercy give service to the community, and as each of them bears witness to the truths of Orthodoxy, it gradually restores the individual to his original state, before the injury of sin. The Russian Church is a living organism, a society of believers all closely involved in the whole of contemporary Soviet society. Even today, pilgrimage to the shrines of Orthodoxy remains important in the lives of the Orthodox faithful, who sometimes travel across the country in search of spiritual comfort and guidance, waiting endlessly at the cell of some nationally revered elder or priest. Now, whenever social problems have intensified, every member of the Church finds himself faced with the question of where he stands not only in religious matters but also on contemporary social issues. Here, the spiritual experience of Orthodox pastors should be considered for its revelance to social life. In this regard, as well as in many others, the Church teaches that we must be guided by the fact that "the human element in the ecclesiastical approach to social history is the source of possible errors in the Church's social teachings," to quote from a 1966 statement issued by Metropolitan Nikodim of Leningrad (d. 1978). The Russian Orthodox Church has a moral and patriotic duty to instill within the young, as well as in members of other generations, a conscientious civic responsibility, moral fortitude, qualities of sacrifice, and fervent service to the interests of society and to those of their contemporaries. Orthodoxy teaches that personal sin is the greatest social evil and affects more than the individual. Thus, sin should be avoided, not just the suffering that it causes, for the disease must be cured, not just the symptoms.

Monasticism has always been the respository—the spiritual foundation and support—of Orthodox purity, and it attracts believers to this very day. Even now, in the second half of the 20th century, a number of important hermits, pastors, preachers, and elders are to be found scattered across the Russian land. Several figures stand in the forefront of the national and religious consciousness of modern Russia: the Trinity–Saint Sergiy Lavra Archimandrites Hegumen Zakharia (d. 1936), Dorimedont, and Serafim (d. 1958); Hierodeacon Varnavi Kukshi (1875–1964), who was Hegumen of the Dormition Monastery in Odessa; Archimandrite Kosma of the Valaam Monastery (d. 1967); Sevastian (d. 1966) and Amvrosiy (d. 1979) of Optina Hermitage; the tireless preacher and national teacher Archimandrite Tavrion (1899–1978) of the

Hermitage of the Savior at Elgava; the elders of Pskov-Pechery Monastery, Simeon and Luke; and from Pochaev Lavra, Iosif, the Archimandrite Andronik (d. 1974) and Serafim (d. 1973), who fulfilled their mission in Tbilisi. But there are and have been many others, either famous or hidden in anonymity from the rest of the world.

The Russian Orthodox Church now has eighteen residential monasteries, in addition to the Gorneye Convent near Jerusalem. The 1920s and 1930s, here and abroad, saw the emergence of "monasticism in the world," a mass movement whose members, both visibly and behind the scenes, sought to confess the Christian faith to the contemporary world. The most important of these witnesses was the much-respected Mother Maria (E. Iu. Kuzmina-Karavaeva), who lived in Paris.

The development of religious instruction has been well served by the seminaries and academies of Moscow, Leningrad, and Odessa. To aid this instruction, the Moscow Patriarchate has since the late 1950s published four editions of the Bible and three of the New Testament, putting out new editions of almost all liturgical books. Since 1943 it has also issued religious calendars and the monthly *Journal of the Moscow Patriarchate* (now published in both Russian and English). And *Theological Works*, a monthly collection, has appeared since 1959.

The contemporary theological activity of the Russian Orthodox Church is marked by the important work of Father Pavel Florenskiy and Professor V.N. Lossky (1903–58), who worked within the traditions established at the beginning of the century by such theologians as Archbishop Vasily (Krivoshein) of Brussels and Belgium; Metropolitan Nikodim (Rotov; d. 1978) of Leningrad and Novgorod; Archbishop Professor Pitirim (Nechaev) of Volokolamsk; Archbishop Mikhail of Vologda and Velikiyustyug; Metropolitan Antoniy of Surozh; Metropolitan Nikolai

(Iarushevich; d. 1961) of Krutitsy and Kolomna; Bishop Afanasiy (Sakharov; d. 1962) of Vladimir; Archpriests M.K. Speransky and A.A. Vetelev (d. 1976); Archpriest Professor L.A. Voronov and Archpriest Professor T.D. Popov (d. 1973); Protopresbyter V. Borovoi; M.A. Starokadomsky (d. 1973); Professors K.E. Skurat, V.D. Sarychev, D.P. Ogitsky, N.A. Zabolotsky, A.I. Georgievsky, A.I. Ivanov (d. 1977), S.V. Troitsky (d. 1972), N.D. Uspensky, K.M. Komarov, A.I. Sagarada, and S.A. Kupressov, among others. Academic theology also drew upon important achievements made by secular scholars, such as A.F. Losev, the historian of philosophy who examined the process by which Christian ideology spread during antiquity and Hellenic times; S.S. Averintsev, a leading Byzantinist; Academician D.S. Likhachev, a major researcher in early Russian culture; Academicians V.N. Lazarev and M.V. Alpatov, both renowned specialists in the field of Russian and Byzantine medieval art.

According to the great Russian writer Fyodor Dostoyevsky, "if a nation retains within itself the ideal of Beauty and requires it...this would assure the greater development of that nation." The Russian Orthodox Church has for a thousand years preserved the rich, living heritage of Russian artistic culture and has been an active force behind its present growth. The heavy damage inflicted upon the cultural monuments of Russia during the Civil War and the revolutionary developments leading to the formation of the Soviet government, not to mention the notoriously destructive period of World War II, gave rise in the 1950s and 1960s to a massive cultural movement intent upon restoring these priceless national treasures. The Russian Orthodox Church actively joined with the Soviet government and society in reclaiming the nation's cultural heritage. A complete return to the monuments of Russian culture, including religious culture, proved especially strong in the postwar period.

The Russian Orthodox Church has helped finance the restoration of a number of unique monuments, a process begun in the 1960s and 70s by the All-Russian Society for the Preservation of Cultural and Historical Monuments. In recent years many ancient churches and monasteries have been resurrected from ruin and neglect. Massive efforts by the scientific and religious community to restore old frescoes and icons led to a rebirth within the Church of the great, long-lost traditions of early Russian pictorial art. Such famous masters as Archbishop Sergiy and Archimandrite Alipiy, V.A. Komarovsky, Hieromonk Grigory, Priest Anatoliy Volgin, N.D. and V.M. Savinykh, and L.A. Uspensky (of Paris) all continue to work surrounded by a host of talented youth, as did M.N. Sokolova who died in 1981.

The men's choir of the Trinity–Saint Sergiy Lavra and the Pochaev Lavra, the women's choir of the Piukhtitsy Convent of the Dormition, talented religious composers and precentors like V.A. Aleksandrov (d. 1962) of Moscow's Saint Nicholas Church in Khamovniki, I.S. Danilov (d. 1971) of the Moscow Theological Academy, V.S. Komarov (d. 1974) of Moscow's Epiphany Cathedral, Archimandrite Matfei of the Trinity–Saint Sergiy Lavra, and N.V. Matveyev of the Transfiguration Church in Moscow have all renewed the great choral tradition of contemporary church music by a return to the monuments of Russian Church music, a rich source also exploited by a host of secular composers, among them G.V. Sviridov. The most important proponents of this heritage have been A.A. Iurlov (1927–73), director of the Academic Chapel Choir of the Russian Republic, M.V. Brazhnikov, who was responsible for deciphering the ancient "hooked" notation of 16th–18th-century Russian religious music and N.N. Pomerantsev, who recorded the bells of the Rostov Kremlin and several other major Russian monasteries. In literature and journalism, this movement to rediscover the achievements of Russia's thousand-year-old culture has manifested itself in the work of a number of young writers and poets, especially in the postwar era.

The history of the Russian Orthodox Church reveals the continuous creativity of God-Man. At every turn, even the most inscrutible events are blessed with the influence of Divine Providence on earth. The historical existence of the Russian Church now approaches its millennium. Ten centuries ago, in the year of ancient Rus' conversion, there occurred a mystical "birth from on high," which gave life, through the Orthodox Church, to a Russian national culture. Among the special gifts that came with this epiphany was the "gift of heraldry," the power to evince the truths of Christ's teaching and to inspire a sense of the blessedness on earth. A thousand years of

Russian religious culture have been invested with the Beauty of preaching, the summoning of the faithful to the "Heavenly life" here below, and this Beauty continues within the collective memory of the greatest Orthodox shrines.

It is not, however, the earthly house of God that has strengthened the Church through all ages, but rather the Church's constant inner struggle, its suffering and torment, and the voluntary sacrifice in the name of Christ. The believing nation of Russia has lived and will continue to live through the immutable "joys of the spirit and mind," joys from God, and will continue to follow the Apostolic commandment: "Rejoice evermore. Pray without ceasing. In everything give thanks: for this is the will of God in Christ Jesus concerning you" (I Thessalonians 5:16–18).

18 Archibishop Serapion of Vladimir and Suzdal during the liturgy in the Cathedral of the Assumption in Vladimir. He is blessing with the Tririkon and the Dirikon (see caption for Plate 4).

19–20 *The Last Judgment,* a fresco by Andrei Rublyov and Daniil Chernyi in the central nave of the Cathedral of the Assumption in Vladimir (1408). The original passages within the painting that remain intact can easily be distinguished from the restorations made in the 19th century.

21 A view of the Bishop's throne during a reading from the Acts of the Apostles in the Cathedral of the Assumption in Vladimir. Officiating at the service is Archbishop Serapion. The frescoes behind him were painted in the 19th century.

22 Archibishop Pitirim of Volokolamsk in the village of Vozmisce in the diocese of Volokolamsk, which is part of the Moscow Eparchy.

23–26 Liturgy during *svyatiky,* or Christmas time, in the Church of the Birth of the Virgin Mary in Vozmisce.

27–30 Christmas celebration in the parish house at Vozmisce.

31 On the way to the Church of the Protection and Intercession of the Virgin Mary in Volokolamsk: "From night till morn my spirit strives towards you, O my Lord."

32 A quiet street in the old section of Volokolamsk. Two priests are on their way to visit parishioners.

33 The Kremlin of Suzdal. On the left is the 13–16th-century Cathedral of the Birth of the Virgin Mary.

34 *Kideksa* at Suzdal. Left of center: the bell tower and the Church of Saint Stefan; right of center: the Cathedral of the Holy Martyrs Boris and Gleb (1152). The church and the cathedral at Peraslavl-Zalessky are the oldest stone churches in Northeast Russia. Kideksa was a Prince's castle at the time the cathedral was built.

35 The Monastery of the Protection and Intercession of the Virgin Mary in Suzdal, founded in 1364. The present structure was erected in the 16th, 17th, and 18th centuries.

36–38 The interior of Trinity Church of the Ipation Monastery in Kostroma (1650–52), its walls frescoed in 1685 by Guriy Nikitin and Sila Savin.

39 The Russian Orthodox Church holds an especially solemn baptism on the eve of Epiphany and on January 6, the feast day itself. Here we see the Great Baptism ceremony with holy water in front of the Church of Saints Constantine and Helen (1707) in Suzdal.

40–45 The Orthodox Church regards the Great Baptism at Epiphany as prototypical of the mysterious washing away of all sins, and also as an actual healing of the nature of water. The priest consecrates the water with incense, reads from the New and Old Testaments, and utters a prayer commemorating all the benefits bestowed by the Lord on humanity. He asks for the Lord's blessing and prays that the water may acquire the power to cleanse and heal body and soul and protect them from evil calumny. The water is blessed three times. At the third blessing the cross is dipped thrice into the water, while the community sings the troparion of the feast. Subsequently, each member of the community receives some of the consecrated water to sprinkle around his house or apartment on that day. At one time the water also served as a means of communion for penitents.

46–47 Although it is bitterly cold in Central Russia at Epiphany (the thermometer registering minus 20°C when this photograph was made), the faithful wait until after the end of the service in order the kiss the cross that had blessed the water.

48–51 The Russian Orthodox Church has a rule that children should be baptized within eight days after their birth. Although it has become difficult to maintain this tradition, Orthodox families still do everything possible to have their newborn baptized at an early date. The physical baptism—like the spiritual baptism symbolized by anointing the child (confirmation)—is carried out in the church itself, or in the baptistery adjacent to the church, with three dips in the water. The spiritual baptism out of the water resembles a second birth and represents a gracious renewal of the entire being. In this way the newborn babe becomes a member of the Church and a member of the body of Christ. As a sign of his or her acceptance into the Church, the neophyte receives a symbolic tonsure (Plate 51).

52 Only civil marriage is legally valid in Soviet Russia. Nonetheless, many couples have a church wedding too. During this service a crown, with a picture of the Savior, is placed on the bridegroom's head and a crown with the picture of the Virgin Mary on the bride's head. Thus, the marriage ceremony is also called the "crowning." The crowns symbolize the dignity and purity of marriage, as well as the respect that the couple owe one another, for each of the partners is the other's crown. But the crowns also signify the nobility of the human being who has been called to create new life.

53 During the marriage ceremony the bride and bridegroom kiss an icon that has been consecrated by the priest. This then becomes their house icon.

54 The Russian Orthodox custom of bearing the dead to church for lying in state continues to be observed whenever possible today. Hymns of consolation are sung above the coffin and a passage from the Gospel of Saint John (5:24–30) is read: "Verily, verily, I say unto you, the dead shall hear the voice of the Son of God; and they that hear shall live. I say unto you, he that heareth my word, and believeth on Him that sent me, hath everlasting life, and shall not come into condemnation; but is passed from death unto life....and shall come forth; they that have done good, unto the resurrection of life." In prayers and songs the faithful ask God to grant the deceased peace of soul in the habitations of the just. The text of the prayer for the remittance of sins is placed in the folded hands of the departed.

55 The Kremlin of Pskov, its fortified ramparts dating back to the 15th century, and the Trinity Church. It was on this spot in the 9th century that Grand Duchess Olga, now venerated as a Saint and an Equal of the Apostles, built the first Russian church dedicated to the Holy Trinity.

56 During the liturgy the faithful hand in slips of paper on which they ask for good health, and also for commemoration and intercession on behalf of deceased relatives. Here a protodeacon and a sexton order the slips before they are read during the litanies.

57 Along with the requests on paper, the petitioners offer *prosfora*. With the words "Remember, O Lord, those who have brought them and those in whose memory they are brought," the priests cut a piece from each *prosfora*. It can happen that the faithful submit so many *prosforae* that several priests are kept busy cutting the pieces while celebrants read off the petitions throughout the entire service.

58 Metropolitan John of Pskov and Pochaev, one of the oldest Hierarchs of the Russian Orthodox Church, here celebrates the liturgy in Trinity Cathedral, Pskov.

59 On Pentecost Saturday the Orthodox Church holds a memorial service for all dead believers who are already part of the Heavenly Church. The faithful bring all kinds of food to this service, which corresponds to what Roman Catholics call All Souls. After placing the food on tables, where the priest blesses it, the parishioners distribute the offerings among themselves or take the victuals home to eat in the company of their friends, in this way commemorating their departed loved ones and relatives. The tradition is rooted in an ancient practice of the Apostolic Church, which was to offer in memory of the deceased a *kolyba*, a sweet made of wheat grains cooked with fruit. The Russian equivalent, *kutsja*, consists of rice, raisins, and syrup. Wheat and rice are both symbols of life, for the deceased go on living in eternity; "Verily, verily, I say unto you, Except a corn of wheat fall into the ground and die, it abideth alone; but if it die, it bringeth forth much fruit" (John 12:24).

60 Inside the Kremlin of Suzdal. At the left is the Church of the Transfiguration (1756); at the right the Church of the Resurrection (1776). Kremlin, a term frequently encountered in Russia, generally refers to the fortified part of the inner city that was originally built by the Princes.

61 The Island of Kizi in Lake Ladoga. At the left is the Church of the Protection and Intercession of the Virgin Mary (1764); at the right the Church of the Transfiguration (1714). The Russian fur trade in the north and northeast was concentrated on Kizi Island in the 17th and 18th centuries. Wealthy businessmen donated churches, which were built of wood, bringing about a golden age of Russian wood architecture. The churches in Kizi are now museums.

62–63 The Church of the Transfiguration in Kizi. With its 22 shingle-covered onion spires built without a single nail, the church is regarded as the outstanding example of Russian wood architecture.

64 The Kremlin at Rostov Veliky. At left the Cathedral of the Assumption (16th century) with the "Hell Wall" (1682–87); at right the west wall and towers (late 12th century) and the Church of the Ascension (1670).

65 The cupolas of the churches in the Rostov Kremlin (16th–17th century).

66 Rostov Veliky: the Spaso-Jakovlevsky (Jacob the Redeemer) Monastery built from the 17th century through the 19th.

67 Russian churches tended to be the focal points of trade and migration at all times. Here we see the arcades of the Cathedral of Rostov Veliky. Traders and artisans used to have their shops in these arcades. The woman in the foreground is selling *kvas*.

19

23
◁22

24

25

26

27–29

42

43

44

45

Archimandrite Longin of Düsseldorf

THE CHURCH ARCHITECTURE OF OLD RUSSIA

In a single instant God gave to the Russian people, just as they were emerging from the depths of paganism, a spiritual insight equal to that of the holy men of Byzantium who were long experienced in ecclesiastical wisdom. In the 8th century Patriarch Herman of Constantinople had clearly defined the nature of the Orthodox Church as "an earthly Heaven in which God lives and dwells." Similar words would be uttered by the emissaries of Prince Vladimir, who, albeit unschooled in theological concepts, were quick to grasp the truth of God. Centuries later we are amazed yet at the enlightenment of these sons of Kievan Rus, who wholeheartedly chose Orthodoxy after visiting a number of different countries: "We came to the Greeks, and they led us to the place where their God dwelt, and we did not know whether we were in Heaven or on earth, because nowhere on earth is there such beauty. We only knew that God Himself dwelt there with His people, and that their [church] ceremony was the best in all the lands."

Christianity jolted the religious consciousness of pagan Russia whose pantheon of differentiated gods symbolized the alienation of the world. The newly converted Russian had to be confused, thirsting as he was for the harmony of all living things in God. For this reason, the difficult theological concept of *Sophia*—that "Divine Wisdom" which brings order to the world—offered Christian Russia the most telling expression of its new spiritual reality. It could hardly be coincidental that while the first white stone church built by Prince Vladimir was dedicated to the Dormition of the Blessed Mother

(989–996), the major cities of the time—Kiev, Polotsk, and Novgorod—erected their first cathedrals in the name of Holy Wisdom.

When Russians began building churches, the material they used was generally logs. A 12th-century Pskov manuscript (the *Ustav* or "Rule") records the earliest known designs for Russian churches. It shows the very kind of colonnaded church that would continue to be erected even during later periods of Russian wood architecture. And the tent roof—actually a tower—would have presented no great problem for local carpenters skilled in putting up wooden military fortresses. Wood served even for the first Russian cathedral, Saint Sophia of Novgorod (late 10th century), a structure large enough that later it would be called "the church with thirteen tops [*verkhi*]."

An Orthodox church represents the duality of existence, its dual form and content foreshadowing—through size, geometry, and color—the duality of earth and Heaven, body and soul, the human and the divine.

"The form or appearance of the church was subjected to symbolism and theology, the better to create a new and unique art filled with inner purpose," wrote the famous archaeologist N.V. Pokrovsky, in a characterization that is quite just. It would be no exaggeration to say that when the Church fathers and scholars laid the foundation of Orthodox archaeology, they did so with a theological understanding of symbolism. Indeed, it was the patristic spiritual heritage and the theological speculation of the Russian Church that gave birth to Russian religious architecture and produced its appearance and symbolism, thereby embuing the church with specific meaning symbolic of the image of the Lord, the image of the universe as blessed by the Holy Spirit, and the image of the communality of the earthly and Heavenly church.

world, but the combination of gold and white should not be thought of merely as a distinguishing sign, for, above all else, the two colors express profound sacred ideas.

In the "Book of the Shepherd" (*Pastyr*) by

Cathedral of Hagia Sofia, Kiev. 1037–61. View of the east side with the original brickwork exposed.

Color is the most important formal element in Russian Church art, whether it be the icon, the applied arts, or even architecture itself. Strange as it may seem, color precedes form in the church architecture of Russian Orthodoxy. Color permits us to recognize a church however obscured it may be by an age-old accumulation of secular buildings or by landscape. There is no mistaking that white spot crowned with the golden spark of a cupola. Even if the form of the church is not discernible several miles away, the nature of the building can be recognized by the illumination the color brings to everything around it. The white paint and gold helmet make a statement to the

Hermas (2nd century), the Church is depicted as a virgin dressed in white. Dionysius the Areopagite called white the symbol of godliness, sincerity, and tranquility. The anonymous Russian author of the "Essay on the Meaning of Signs, Standards, and Insignias" tells us that white is the color of "the absence of hatred, honesty, purity of conscience, truth, that which is nondecaying, complete, and immaculate." While wide in latitude, this interpretation offers a precise symbolism for the color white, something that would not escape the attention of Russian artists and architects of the day. At first, the application of this principle was somewhat restrained. In its early stages, Russian church style adhered to the Byzantine tradition of a decorative, rhythmic approach to the building surface, showing a preference for bare brick or stone masonry. As the Russian Church became more autonomous, the tradition of uncovered

from both a decorative and a symbolic point of view. Glistening from afar, the Russian church produced a truly enchanting effect on the earthly viewer, as it struck his eye among the gray hovels of the city or in the fallow environment of nature.

Church of Mary the Protectress and Guardian. Bogoljubovo. 1165. View from the west.

masonry gradually gave way to the custom of whitewashing church walls. In time, practically all stone churches in Russia, even those constructed during periods of strong Byzantine influence, would be white. The utilization of white stone taken from native quarries and the practice of whitewashing walls proved the most effective means of treating the church's outer surfaces,

Gold has been as important a religious symbol as white and for just as long, but with greater significance. The scarcity, nobility, and value of gold, its likeness to the sun guaranteed that the precious metal would make an early appearance in Christian history, especially during that initial era of the "golden symbol." One of the first churches constructed after the legalization of the Church in Roman times was the Church of the Holy Apostles in Constantinople (337), which had a golden cupola and subsequently became a prototype for the majority of Eastern Orthodox churches. Yet, atop the churches of Byzantium,

eternal life, immortality, preciousness, sovereignty, light, brilliance, and, above all else, divinity. Russian architects would therefore always crown their church buildings with gold. And it became a tradition—golden cupolas over the white stone

Cathedral of Saint Dimitriy, Vladimir. 1193–97. View from the south.

gold was more the exception than the rule, unlike the situation in Russia, where gilded domes became commonplace. According to the *Kormchaia Kniga*, "the top of the church is the head of Our Lord." Such an exalted interpretation of the church's summit could hardly be satisfied with a simple tower. Symbolically, only gold would do, with all its connotations of exclusivity,

walls of a church, or over white stone masonry covered with whitewash—giving the Russian church its unique appearance and affecting the look of every Russian town. It is hardly surprising, therefore, that poets and writers, wishing to convey the visual character of old Moscow, would use such the epithets as "topped with gold" or "with walls of white."

Geometric forms also play an important role in the appearance and expressive language of the Russian church. The most important of these are the square and the circle.

The allegorical interpretation of the square

found in the fifth book of the *Stromateis* of Clement of Alexandria, one of the Church's early teachers. Invested with this symbolic value, the square would provide the plan for the foundation of the Orthodox church. The square became both

Trinity–Saint Sergiy Lavra, Zagorsk. 1422–23. View from the northeast.

dates back to antiquity (Plato saw the "true" man as "square"), but the full meaning of the square as an image was not articulated until Christian times, when the right angles and equal sides of the form came to signify correctness, organization, tranquility, equality, calm, and, therefore, the rectitude of that which is represented by the square. "Righteousness is square" is a statement

the symbol and the receptacle of the church.

The circle yielded another important element of church design. Here the symbolism is particularly rich, for as a continuous form with neither beginning nor end, the circle stood for eternity. Contemplating the closed form and unbroken line of the circle, the Church fathers discovered within the image a great store of spiritual implications. As a symbol of timelessness, infinity, nonbeginning, and nonending, the circle proved to be a theologically sound guide for church construction, in that it constituted the most complete and precise symbolic re-creation

without or from within, the Russian Orthodox church invariably appears as a square joined to a semicircle, if only in the dome that crowns and blesses it.

The Russian Church's love for and loyalty to

Cathedral of the Assumption in the Moscow Kremlin. 1475–79.
View from the south.

of the image of the Divinity. Architects, attentive to the voice of theologians, followed this guide to the fullest, crowning every elevation over a square-plan church with a circular form—the "Heavenly circle." Whether it be a cupola or a drum, the image would express the Divine in space and form.

In Russian religious architecture, the square symbolizes mankind and the earthly Church. At no time does the square close in on itself; instead, it always opens into a semicircle. Observed from

the dome may seem surprising, especially so if we consider the structural difficulties it poses. But the devotion is justified, since the semicircle serves to re-create one of the most profound images of Christian theology: God in the world, Jesus Christ, Heaven reaching down to earth. If the enclosed square can be seen as a symbol of the world, centered around itself and bound by its own limitations, and the circle as a symbol of God, complete within Himself, then Russian architecture must find a way to open these lines to each other, imposing cohesive unity on that which is difficult to unite. The circle within the square fulfills that ideal, especially close to the Russian heart, of the inseparability of the material and the spiritual, of the relationship of God and man.

stands for the Blessed Mother, who unites Heaven and earth by opening the path leading to salvation. The anonymous 16th-century Russian author of *The Seven Names of Mary* lists the door as an essential attribute of the Mother-Guide.

Church of the Ascension in Kolomenskoye, Moscow. 1530–32.

The doors leading into a church have a semicircular top. Three in number, they symbolize the Holy Trinity, a tradition that began with the construction of the first Christian church, as described by Eusebius of Caesarea. Within the symbolic system of the Orthodox Church, moveover, the door is associated with the Blessed Virgin, for by symbolizing "the Gates of Jerusalem," that most ancient of symbols, it also

Seen from afar, as a dark silhouette against the white walls of the church, the doors, each topped with its semicircular form, recall the *maforiia* (from the Greek *maphorion* for headdress) of the Mother of God, whose patronage extends to all believers.

In the upper walls of the church the tall, narrow windows with their semicircular tops have a feminine quality that artists and architects have always associated with holy women. The concept is reinforced by the icon painter who not only places the image of the Virgin over the church door but also includes certain women revered for their sanctity among the images frescoed on the walls of church interiors.

Everything planned and materialized in the form of the church becomes an actual reality at the altar, that repository of grace which lights the way of the ecclesiastical ship as it moves from vale to mountain. The great spiritual destiny of the Church is revealed and realized at the altar. There are two high points in the Russian Orthodox church: the cupola and the altar. We know the first from visual experience, but the second can be apprehended only through inspiration. The altar constitutes the spiritual summit of the church, and its symbolism is integral with the semicircular system found in every Russian church, where the dome over the altar apse is semicircular, as is the altar apse itself. The abundance of semicircular forms at the altar is no accident, since it draws attention to the special spiritual meaning of this place, the "earthly paradise," through which Heaven descends to and covers the earth.

All Christian churches tend to be symbolically tall. But when examining the height of the Russian church, specialists do so only within the context of the surrounding buildings or landscape. Compared to the low cottages and villas in which the people of Old Russia lived, the Orthodox church truly seems to stand quite tall. In absolute terms, the Russian church is not tall, although traditionally it is built on high ground, in order to appear lofty and removed. Its classical square or cubic design limits the height, for a twofold purpose: While striving to reach on high, the church remains firmly on the ground.

This duality of meaning also extends to spatial relationships. If the voice of reason tells the architect that God is far off, then his heart must tell him that He is near. Actually, God is remote

only to those who for one reason or another find themselves outside the walls of the church. The believer feels Him close at hand, which the spiritual experience of the Holy Eucharist justifies. Personal spirituality and long contemplation concerning God had its effect on Russian architects, who built churches that were tall relative to their surroundings, yet not tall in and of themselves. As a matter of principle, one's understanding of God should not inspire awe or fear. God should not be approached on tiptoes. Religious architecture is but one way in which the Russian Church expresses this attitude.

The special relationships of space and the geometrical, numerical, and color symbolism are canonical elements of Russian Orthodox Church architecture. Still, it would not be correct to view architectural canon as static. For Rus, canon was not a burden, but a support, and nowhere in Russia does one find two exact icons or two exact churches. The overall trend of Russian religious architecture makes it impossible to speak of a slavish devotion to canon. Church builders loved the canon but combined it with a sensitive attention to local needs of material, time, and place. Much as stone came into use, many churches continued to be built with wood, a material not only less safe but also less flexible, since it largely prohibits semicircular forms. The favorite finish for the exterior of churches was whitewash and gold, but to this day there are many churches in Russia with rich, multicolored decorations, as well as a multitude of undecorated wooden churches. Herein lies another manifestation of the Russian church builder's concern for local materials and needs. Although the square provided the form most favored for foundations, architectural history has disclosed a number of cruciform plans, as well as elongated and polyhedron shapes. The five-domed plan (symbolizing Christ and the four Evangelists) proved very attractive and became a tradition, but construction practices indicate that this, the most prominent type allowed by canon, was often replaced by other dome systems offering a suitable numerical symbolism, from that of the single dome (signifying the Unity of the Divine

such national importance as the construction of churches there would be no room for an art reared on strict dogma.

"The Church fathers established not only liturgical rite for the church, but also its outer

Cathedral of Saint Basil on Red Square, Moscow. 1555–60.
View from the southwest.

Substance) to structures with thirty-three domes (one for each of the years in Christ's earthly life).

In Old Russia everyone took part in church construction. Sometimes the faithful would raise a church in one day. This centuries-old tradition, in which all of society (Tsars, Boyars, and peasants) played a part, gave the Russian church that unforgettable look, with its striking multitude of diverse forms. It is only natural that in a matter of

construction and inner appearance as well, foretelling all, foreseeing all," wrote the Most Holy Patriarch Aleksiy (d. 1970). With these words the Patriarch briefly summed up the essence of Russian church architecture and its deeply thought-out symbolism, which took form not in isolation, but in close relationship to patristic tradition, and with the foresight of the highest Church authorities. It would be appropriate to recall that the Russian Church was enjoined from ancient times to construct churches "in accordance with the rules of the Holy Apostles and the Holy Fathers." Nurtured and fed on patristic thought, the church building itself came to embody this idea in stone. The spiritual vision of the Church fathers, profoundly sensed and experienced by the Russian nation, the synthesis of thought and action, the "thoughtful action"—herein lies the key to understanding the nature of Russian spiritual creativity. It is the unfading power and beauty of Russian church architecture that allows it to become an example of noble simplicity, of depth and clarity, so long as it retains its functional and aesthetic dignity. It consitutes an art in which nothing is accidental, and while not technically precise, the Russian church is inspired by and embued with the highest ideals. During his life, the Russian philosopher Prince E. Trubetskoi called the icon "theological speculation in colors." By the same token Russian church architecture could be called "theological speculation in stone."

68 Students of the Moscow Theological Academy at the beginning of their term.

69 Admission examination at the Leningrad Theological Academy. More and more frequently these days, Russians who have completed their university degrees are choosing to seek spiritual careers.

70–73 The solemn but merry, and also somewhat sad, day when the theological students graduate, an occasion on which friends and relatives are allowed to participate in the celebration. The scene here is at Zagorsk.

74 It is an old tradition for the students at the Moscow Theological Academy in Zagorsk to move in procession to Trinity Church and there ask for a blessing from the founder of the monastery, Saint Sergiy of Radonezh.

75 Here, during graduation at the Moscow Theological Academy, Patriarch Pimin hands each graduate his diploma. At the right of the Patriarch is the Rector of the Moscow Theological Schools and Archbishop of Dmitrov, Vladimir. At the Patriarch's left is his deputy in the Trinity–Saint Sergiy Lavra at Zagorsk, Archimandrite Hieronymus.

76–78 A class for conductors at the Leningrad Theological Academy. In recent years the Moscow and Leningrad Theological Academies have introduced classes for church choir leaders in which women may enroll while they also study theology and Church history, in preparation for practical activities in their churches.

79–84 Bishop Meliton of Tichvin celebrates the liturgy in Trinity Cathedral at Leningrad while also ordaining a student of the Leningrad Theological Academy for the priesthood.

85 Professors and students at the Moscow Theological Academy on the final day of their spring 1981 term.

70

71

73

72

74
75▷

85

Leonid Uspensky

ICONS
AND FRESCOES

Russian religious art possesses a very special beauty, a beauty whose purpose and effect are to disclose evangelical truths. It could hardly be otherwise, for in the words of one Church historian, "the beginnings of Russian Christianity constituted an unprecedented impulse, comparable to that of the primitive Church of Jerusalem, to fulfill the evangelical ideal."[1] It is significant that the acceptance of this ideal was made possible by visual and tangible forms of art.

Byzantine missionary activity in Russia became especially intense during the period immediately following Orthodoxy's struggle with and ultimate victory over iconoclasm. The renewal of faith in the efficacy of images produced a veritable renaissance in the art created for the Orthodox Church, and the energy embodied in that art was a quality to which Byzantium attached the utmost importance. We may therefore assume that Byzantine missionaries made a special effort to introduce Orthodox art, with all its new-found force and conviction, among the recently converted. A letter of Saint Photius, the Patriarch of Constantinople, to the Bulgarian Emperor Basil, includes the decisions by the Seventh Universal Council in regard to the teaching of the Orthodox faith, a process in which icon veneration was to be given preference over other methods.[2] According to the chronicles the decisive factor in the conversion of Prince Vladimir to Christianity was his being shown an icon of the Last Judgment. Thus, even legend reflects the great value placed upon the power of icons.

It is especially important for Russian Church art and its urgent content that ancient Rus embraced Christianity at the very moment when Byzantium itself was experiencing spiritual rebirth, a movement that reached its climax during the life of Simeon the New Theologian. The religious art that came forth in Byzantium at this time proved to be the most highly developed of any then to be found in Europe. And it gave to Russia the *Bogoroditse*, or "Mother of God Icon," that incomparable jewel now universally known as the *Virgin of Vladimir*.

Drawing on patristic teaching and figurative traditions, Russian Church art evinced a standard of antique harmony and measured sensibility that became part of the living fabric of Russian society.

If the Byzantine heritage could be so rapidly absorbed into Russian art, it was thanks to the readiness or prepared state of the native Russian culture. Recent studies have confirmed that the art of pagan Rus was highly developed—and, moreover, less antithetical to Christianity than had been the art of classical antiquity. The pagan art of Rus, for instance, displayed nothing of the illusionism, or naturalism, that had been the hallmark of the Greco-Roman tradition, all so alien to the Christian's spiritualized view of the world. For those early Russian converts to Christianity, a nonillusionistic art posed no problem whatever.

Cultural exchange accelerated the process of conversion, resulting in a fruitful collaboration between Russian and Byzantine masters. The freshly converted nation proved fully capable of

[1] A.V. Kartashev, *Ocherki po istorii Russkoi Tserkvi (Essays on the History of the Russian Church)*, Paris, 1959, Vol. I, p. 129.

[2] Glavy (chapters 18–20), Patr. Gr. 102, column 649–656.

above: Saint Luke, from the *Ostomirov Gospel.* 11th century.

left: The Virgin of Vladimir. Byzantine icon. Early 12th century. Tretyakov Gallery. Moscow.

assimilating the Byzantine heritage, which would never find so favorable a climate or achieve such splendid results as in Russia.

No better proof of Russia's affinity for the great art of Orthodoxy can be found than in the fact that the Russian Church instituted a liturgical holiday (February 14) in memory of the twelve Greek architects and artists who built and decorated the Cathedral of the Dormition at Kiev-Pechery Lavra, ending their lives there wearing monks' habits.

The first reference to Russian painters occurs in the 11th century, when the *Kiev-Pechery Paterik*

cites two students, Saints Alimpiy and Grigoriy, both monks of the Kiev-Pechery Lavra, who had been trained by Greek masters. The *Paterik* also mentions other painters, but without giving either their names or their social status. We know little about the work of Alimpiy and Grigoriy, although tradition attributes to Alimpiy the *Pechery Virgin,* an icon that includes portraits of Saints Antoniy and Feodisy, abbots of the monastery, then at the very center of Russian spiritual life. The same tradition holds that the painting was executed in 1085.

Saints Alimpiy and Grigoriy lived during what was a period of intense creativity for the Russian

Orthodox Church. The Byzantine heritage had just undergone a radical change, and new forms of artistic expression were being evolved, although few Russian icons associated with the early 12th century display any evidence of recent aesthetic trends within Byzantium. By the 13th century, however, Russian icon painting begins to show signs of an organic assimilation, a unique transformation and understanding of the essence

Virgin Orans, icon from the Monastery of the Savior in Iaroslavl. Tretyakov Gallery, Moscow.

of Christianity. The process can be seen in the wide diversity of masters who flourished in the country's historic political centers during the period of feudal dismemberment, and in the artists' adaptation of local characteristics from one part of the country or another.

No icons have come down to us from the 11th century. Apart from mosaics and murals, the only figural art to survive from that period is in the form of illuminated manuscripts, such as the *Ostromirov Gospel* and the *Anthology (Izbornik)* of Svyatoslav, as well as in some of the minor arts. The earliest Russian icons belong to the 12th and 13th centuries, and to a greater or lesser extent these display local characteristics of color, form, and composition, which specialists trace to Novgorod, Iaroslavl, and Vladimir-Suzdal.

In 1155 Prince Andriy Bogoliubsky transferred the *Virgin of Vladimir* icon from Kiev to the eponymous city of Vladimir, thereby signalling the shift of the nation's political center from the south to the northwest. There, for the veneration of this icon, Bogoliubsky ordered an enormous new cathedral, built in the years 1158–60 and dedicated to the Dormition of the Virgin.

In the 12th century the Russian Church would establish in the region of Vladimir the feast of the Patronage of the Holy Mother of God (*Pokrov Presviatoi Bogoroditsy*), which, although unknown to Byzantium, was based on events that had taken place there. In establishing this feast day, the Church expressed some of the uniquely Russian aspects of Orthodoxy's religious art, especially the passionate veneration of the Virgin Mother as the Patroness of the land. Blessed Prince Andriy Bogoliubsky went on to erect the first church dedicated to the theme of this new feast, the illustrious Church of the Defender at

Nerli, the pearl of Russian architecture. This project undoubtedly led to the corresponding use of the theme in pictorial art, where it attained its present universality. Another Virgin motif that entered icon painting at this time is that of the Virgin Orans (*Bogoliubskaia Ee*), which presents Our Lady petitioning Christ for the benefit of the human race. Although the Feast of the Defender celebrates the Virgin as Patroness of humanity, the service also makes note of her intercession on behalf of the entire world. In lines from "O Lord, hear us," she is cited as "the wondrous defender of the whole world." This theme of global patronage finds its clearest expression in the wonderfully composed, uniquely Russian iconographic theme derived from "O Blessed One, all things rejoice in you...." During the Feast of the Defender service, the icon of the Mother of God assumes universal meaning, as "the Joy of all living things." In the background of a Russian church, gathered about the Mother of God, appear all creatures, both earthly and Heavenly.

The inner and outer décor of the Russian Orthodox church mirrors and extends the liturgical system. More than a place of gathering for worship, the church is a confessor of faith. In other words, it represents Divine Beauty on an earthly plane, becoming an environment where "God dwells with man." Decorated with icons and murals depicting the saints and filled with the sounds of the liturgy, the church—its structure and embellishment—becomes a unified manifestation of the Church of Heaven and Earth. The Russian faithful respond to both the exterior and, more importantly, the interior décor with inimitable fervor. The chronicle descriptions of the churches of Vladimir-Suzdal overflow with love and admiration: "The church is wondrously

decorated with miraculous signs [that is, murals], with holy icons, with books and other precious holy objects, and every kind of splendor."[3]..."and it is decorated with various icons."..."and all who see it speak of its formidable beauty."[4]

Russian art flowered brilliantly from the 11th century to the 13th, only to be interrupted by the Tatar invasions. The Tatars drained Russia, not only physically but culturally, destroying churches and monasteries and driving the masters of various crafts into slavery. But religious life continued, the faith of Russians endured, and the Church survived this tragic time with vigor, as did its art. Indeed, the artistic impulse never faltered, and creativity flowed without a break. The very fact that religion continued meant constant restoration of what had been ruined or destroyed. Cultural output remained vital not only in Novgorod and Pskov, towns that retained their political independence and escaped pillage, but even in those provinces that fell under Tatar domination. Some monasteries and churches kept cells for builders and icon painters, who, between invasions, succeeded in erecting churches and painting icons, albeit at a reduced rate of production relative to what had been possible in the previous period. From this output comes a series of icons, the work of various provinces, that scholars recognize as quite marvelous.

After the initial stagnation induced by Tartar vandalism, Russian Church art entered a period of vitality that extended to all areas of aesthetic activity. In 1325, well before its emergence as the political capital of the nation, Moscow under Metropolitan Pitirim became the spiritual center of All Russia. Guided by the Church's finest representatives, the Saints of Moscow, particularly the Holy Metropolitan Aleksiy and Saint Sergiy Radonezh, the Church achieved a unification of greater Rus that anticipated the nation's political unity. Throughout the internecine struggles of the

---

[3] *Polnoe Sobranie Russkikh Letopisei (Complete Collection of Russian Chronicles)*, XXI (year 1152), p. 192.

[4] *Ibid*, II, p. 681.

Pantokrator, fresco by Feofan the Greek in the dome of the Church of the Transfiguration in Novgorod. 1378.

Detail of an angel in frescoes painted by Daniil Chernyi and Andrei Rublyov for the Cathedral of the Assumption. Vladimir. 1408.

Princes and the devastating Tatar raids, the Church preserved the unity of the Russian lands. Given the unity of Russia's Christian faith, the bickering Princes could not but seem utterly alien to the nature of the Church. The hostility of the time struck all believers as a break with the evangelic norm. Under the protection of the Blessed Mother through her icon, the Russian people saw the Tatars turned back from Moscow on three different occasions.[5]

At this time Rus carried out an intensely active spiritual and cultural life. "During those days it experienced the good news of the Gospels with a force that had never been seen either before or since. In the suffering of Christ it had beheld its own Golgotha, accepting the Resurrection of Christ with joy worthy of hearts that had just been released from Hell."[6] At the end of this road of

[5] In commemoration thereof, the Russian Church established three feasts, on August 26, on June 23, and on May 21. The copy of the *Virgin of Vladimir* made by Andrei Rublyov is now at the Municipal Museum in Vladimir.

[6] E.H. Trubetskoi. *Umozrenie v kraskakh (Theological Speculation in Colors),* Paris; 1965, p. 135.

tribulation, Orthodox Rus rose up purified and enlightened, having become aware of its own power from the process of liberating itself from the Tatar Yoke. Now the creative forces of Rus would reach their greatest fulfillment. Culturally, the nation entered a period of unusual expressiveness, freedom, and directness, with full command of tonal purity and rich, radiant color. This vitality demonstrated the spiritual ascent of a generation raised under the influence of the greatest Russian Saints. Russians now harvested the fruits of national torment, endured over the centuries, and nowhere had the joyfulness and confidence of the Christian message been expressed so clearly as in Russian Church art of this era.

The 14th and 15th centuries witnessed a strong revival of church construction throughout the entire country. As noted previously, the building of churches was the primary method by which Russians could express their national piety. One hundred and fifty new monasteries were erected between 1340 and 1440, and by the end of the 15th century, in Pskov alone, forty churches went up inside monasteries and some twenty took form in the city itself.

Within these newly built stone churches, a number of famous masters participated in covering the walls with murals. In 1374 Feofan the Greek painted the Church of the Savior on Ilin Street in Novgorod. In 1405 Feofan painted the Church of the Annunciation in the Moscow Kremlin, while "assisting the master…was the elder Prokhor of Gorodets and the painter Andrei Rublyov." Of their work in this cathedral, only two tiers of the iconostasis have survived.   In 1408 Rublyov and Daniil Chernyi decorated the newly rebuilt Church of the Dormition in Vladimir. Some fragments of this work survive, most notably a Last Judgment scene and a few icons from the iconostasis, now kept in the Tretyakov Gallery in Moscow and the Russian Museum in Leningrad.

The Three Archangels Appearing to Abraham, painted by Andrei Rublyov for the iconostasis in Trinity Cathedral at Trinity-Saint Sergiy Lavra, Zagorsk. Early 15th century.

Just recently a few mural fragments from the church's original 12th-century construction have been found.

In 1475–79 the well-known Italian architect Aristotle Fioravanti built the new Cathedral of the Dormition in the Moscow Kremlin, which became the seat of the Russian Church and the burial place of the Metropolitans and Patriarchs. The murals here were executed in 1481–82 by the famous master Dionisiys, working with his two sons. A few of the icons have survived, among them a pair representing Metropolitans Pitirim and Aleksiy, both leading Church officials. Other works to survive from the hand of Dionisiys are the large mural, complete and unretouched, from the Cathedral of the Nativity of the Blessed Virgin at Ferapontov Monastery.

By the end of the 14th century the Trinity–Saint Sergiy Monastery had become the spiritual center of Old Russia. Over the course of the century, this monastery, hidden deep in the forest, developed into a crucible for Russia's unity and creative vitality. Here Saint Sergiy built a wooden church dedicated to the Holy Trinity, which he hoped would "dispel the fear and hateful divisiveness from this world." Here also, in 1422, rose the white stone Cathedral of the Holy Trinity, decorated by Andrei Rublyov, Daniil Chernyi, "and others," according to the monastery's Abbot, Nikon, once a student and colleague of Saint Sergiy. The murals having faded, they were painted over in the 17th century; yet Rublyov's iconostasis remained intact, complete with its famous icon of the Trinity. The entire treasure is now at the Tretyakov Gallery in Moscow.

Rublyov also participated in the construction of the white stone Church of the Savior of the Transfiguration (*Spaso-Preobrazhensky*) at the Andronnikov Monastery founded by Metropolitan Aleksiy. Still at work on the murals at the end of his life, the great artist was buried in the church. Unfortunately, neither the burial place nor the frescoes survives. The monastery itself now contains a museum of icons, dedicated to the name of Andrei Rublyov.

If monumental wall painting became the principal form of Russian art in the 11th, 12th, and 13th centuries, in the 15th century it was the icon that offered Russians the chief means of expressing their spiritual and cultural life. The Orthodox conception of beauty received its greatest articulation in icons, their beauty embodying the sanctity of the prototypes—the holy personages portrayed. Russian art of this period evinces a

cohesive unity of doctrinal teaching, the experience of prayer, and creativity. Here was the age that saw a rebirth of Hesychasm in Byzantium, and although Russia did not participate directly in that controversy, the country felt the effects quite deeply. It could be said that if Byzantium acquired its theology through the word, Russia obtained its theology through the image. It was left to Russia to show how artistic language could, within the framework of the icon, realize its maximum potential for spirituality. "With a kind of material confidence, the icon testifies to the depth and complexity, to the genuine wealth, of the early Russian spiritual experience, the creative power of the Russian soul."[7] It was a time when Russian art attained its highest level of creativity when it responded to the demands presented by the Orthodox world view.

From the very outset the Russian Church took an interest in the theological requirements for the icon, and this can be seen in the record of penetrating discussions not only of specific iconographic details but even of entire ensembles. And the Church's preoccupation with icons became especially marked during the period when Russian Church art reached its culminating development. There may be no better demonstration of this than in that most essential accessory of the Russian church service, the iconostasis.

The altar screen that the Russian Church inherited from Byzantium evolved, gradually to be sure, and attained its definitive expression in the 15th century, when the true potential of the form became fully evident. Now the iconostasis would be worked out with all the clarity needed to display its theological content and liturgical form. While no set theme governed the content of church murals, the iconostasis was subject to a

[7] G. Florovsky, *Puti russkogo bogosloviia (The Ways of Russian Theology)*, Paris, 1937, p. 1.

strictly defined and unchanging thematic program. The classic five-tier iconostasis could be seen as a marvelously composed pictorial transposition of the Eucharistic Canon, both in its scope and the terseness of its prayer: "You, and Your only-begotten Son, and Your Holy Spirit, You who called us from nothingness into being, who, having fallen, rose from the dead, and did not abandon all living things, who calls us from this earth to Heaven, and grants us the future of a Heavenly Kingdom." Set forth upon one flat surface directly facing the supplicant, the iconostasis can be seen from any vantage point within the church. Along each tier, it depicts the history of humanity, created in the image of the triune God; His hand in history; the path of man's ascent; the Almighty's redeeming actions for the sake of humankind; the preparation and prophecy of the Old Testament; its fulfillment in the New Testament; the unity of the material and the spiritual worlds; the salvation of the human race; the establishment of the Church; and, finally, God's gift to humanity: the Kingdom of Heaven.

By accepting revelation (the theme of the Holy Gates, meaning evangelical prophecy), by accepting the sacraments (the communion of the Apostles over the Holy Gates), man is raised into the collective body of the Church, the Body of Christ. Within this Eucharistic community, the Church becomes a forerunner of the gift of God, the Kingdom of Heaven. In other words, that which is real but cannot be seen is fulfilled at the altar, all the while that the iconostasis visually depicts this fulfillment, becoming the pictorial manifestation of the Eucharistic Sacrament.

The iconostasis, with its historical continuum, discloses the icon to be the reality of revelation, the reality of the incarnation and redemption. Consequently, it is also visible testimony to the Eucharist, teaching men about this sacrament and illustrating it as well.

From an artistic standpoint, the iconostasis brought to the fore all the laconicism, or terseness, of Russian artistic language. Even in its festive, multifigured icons, there is a simplicity and clarity of placement, a crispness of line, a precision of silhouette, and, of course, powerful color. In its final form, the five-tier iconostasis achieved genuine grandeur. When Feofan the Greek and Andrei Rublyov painted at the Church of the Annunciation in Moscow, they made the icons for their deësis lifesize, an unusually monumental scale for the time. In the Church of the Dormition at Vladimir, Rublyov and Daniil Chernyi enlarged the deësis to 3.14 meters and gave the iconostasis an unprecedented solemnity, monumentality, and expressiveness.

Icon masters concentrated their activity around the monasteries, which became breeding grounds for art and enlightenment. Among the many icon painters of this prolific period, a great number were sons of the Church, such as the Metropolitan Pitirim, Metropolitan Simon, Valaam, Makariy, Athanasiy, and other bishops, priests, monks, and a host of laymen, such as the famous master Dionisiys. The Church canonized many of these masters, thereby confirming the sanctity of their lives.

During the post-Rublyov period, the spiritual preeminence of the icon diminished somewhat, while the formal aspects of figural art assumed greater importance. Still, the 16th century gave the Russian Church some of its finest artistic masterpieces, achieved within the basic direction already laid out and preserving the spiritual wealth, simplicity, and monumental form. By the end of the century icons would appear that, owing to their technical virtuosity and rich materials, assumed the value of luxurious, jeweled handicrafts.

As Russia became unified under a centralized government, local traits of Church art began to lose their independent character and blend into an overall system of national art. Metropolitan Makariy of Moscow, a leading Church figure and himself an icon painter, instituted a Metropolitan workshop for icon production. The widespread veneration of portrait icons at this time is related to Makariy's canonization of a number of previously revered saints.

The Patriarchate's icon workshop and the great majority of icon painters staunchly upheld the Orthodox tradition, even into the 18th century, and continued to display a respectable degree of spirituality and creativity. But the tsarist icon studios developed a taste for Western realism, a trend that led to the beginning of Russian secular art as well as to a secularization of art within the Church and a break with its traditions. Thus, during the 18th and 19th centuries two styles of art coexisted within the Russian Church: that of traditional Orthodoxy, and that derived from the West, which was nothing more than secular figural art with religious themes.

Russian Church art was the living expression of Orthodox faith, and whatever questioned the faith-giving foundations of that art deeply disturbed the Russian people. And so the Church devoutly sought to preserve the purity of the Orthodox icon. The turn away from tradition led to stormy controversy and much anguish in 16th- and 17th-century Russia, more than anywhere else in the Orthodox world. Inevitably, it led to a great deal of bitterness and harm. In the second half of the 16th century, the new tendencies in Church art became a major issue on the agenda of the National Councils of the Russian Church. Among the regulations set down by the Council of One Hundred Chapters (*Stoglav*) of 1551 were a number of rules intended to prevent questionable practices in iconography, while other resolutions dealt with the foundations and principles of icon painting, as well as with the icon painters

themselves. Church art continued to be a topic during the Councils of 1553–54.

In the 17th century, Patriarch Nikon reacted strongly against the new direction then emerging in Russian art. Patriarch Joachim also struggled with this, seeing "a turning away from ecclesiastical tradition." In 1667 the Great Council of Moscow devoted considerable attention to artistic matters, especially the depiction of the Divinity. It categorically forbade the production of any image of God the Father, this being directly contrary to Orthodox teaching. From the period survive some ten examples of polemical, and occasionally abrasive, writing both for and against the new trends. Among the century's monuments is a collection of essays published in 1642 under the title *Tsvetnik*, meaning "Flowerbed," which defended the Orthodox tradition with patristic apologia.

The primary cause of such a violent reaction to change was the Russian believer's special love and reverence for the icon, which, more than anywhere else in the world, gave the people the vivid sensation of being in the very presence of holiness. The icon was perceived as a necessity, not only of spiritual life, but of public life as well. In a nation where society, politics, and the Church were all closely interrelated, the icon was looked to for protection. Political events often called for the construction of a church, or a feast would be established and dedicated to an icon whose miraculous power had been responsible for the outcome of a given situation. The chronicles, when recording events of political importance, also note the erection of churches, their decoration and painting, even the transfer or restoration of icons. The daily life of the common people revolved around feast days and days commemorating the saints. This was especially true of the agricultural calendar. The icon remained with Russians throughout their lives, from the moment of birth to the hour of death.

As already stated, the Mother of God received the greatest reverence as Russia's Patroness, and her nearness to the world has always been keenly felt by the Russian people. ("While we slept, you remained with us, O Mother of God.") Throughout its history the Russian nation has turned to the Holy Mother of God for protection, which she bestowed through her icon, and therein lies the explanation of the widespread appeal of Our Lady icons, especially the *Virgin of Umilenie (Eleusa* in Greek, or "tenderness"). In the esteem of believing Russians, the Blessed Mother's image occupies the most prominent place after the icon of the Savior, and among the icons of the saints, hers receives the most intense devotion and the greatest variety of forms. It should be sufficient to observe that the liturgical ceremony provides 160 names with which to praise the miracles of the icon of the Virgin. Russian literature as a whole contains more than 700 names associated with the icon of the Virgin Mother of God.[8]

Today the icon is central to the impression the world has of the Russian Orthodox Church. Indeed, it could be said that the icon is one of the great artistic and spiritual discoveries made by the 20th century. To non-Russians, it seems to be the most genuine aesthetic means of teaching the Christian faith and life. Certainly, the icon provides the most direct and honest approach for anyone eager to know Orthodoxy, since "the significance of the icon for Orthodox piety and Orthodoxy's theological foundation makes it a path to the most important points of Orthodox doctrine. An

understanding of the icon is an understanding of that which is doctrinally central, and it opens the way to other aspects of theology."[9]

The icon has been the most effective instrument for spreading Orthodoxy, attracting believers by its warmth, its tranquility, and its closeness to the individual. The Russian people, in order to express their faith, created within the Church a great cultural tradition, a tradition without parallel elsewhere in the world. To a confused humanity, this art reveals the existence of the Church within the images of sacred figures and indicates and makes real the possibility for achieving victory over the "hateful divisiveness within this world." The Russian icon clearly expresses the inner harmony of man reconciled with God, with himself, and with his fellow man, doing so through its profound images, its festive beauty, and the power and harmony of its color.

Thanks to many anonymous generations of Russian artists, traditional iconography and pictorial technique have been preserved throughout the centuries. As it builds new churches, restores murals, and paints new icons, this tradition brings resurgent powers to the modern Church. New or old, at any level of craftsmanship, the icon reveals the transience of life, a reality that a distracted world needs to embrace. As in previous centuries, the Church, through its art, continues to announce the joy of salvation brought to mankind and all creation by Christ. This joy manifests not only the power of spiritual life but also a beauty unknown to modern civilization. Through its teaching, the Russian Church fulfills its saving mission on earth, and through its art—the beauty of the icons, the brilliance of their colors—Orthodoxy expresses joy in the pursuit of this goal. Russian religious art brings to the world a splendor that the Church itself received at the dawn of its history, a beauty which, in the words of Dostoyevsky, "saves the world."

---

[8] See the *Mesiatseslov Sergeiia (The Calendar of Sergiy)*, Vol. I, 2nd ed., 1901. This, of course, did not mean that each icon was completely different. The same iconographic type could have many titles associated with the place of origin or actual location.

[9] E. Benz. *Geist und Leben der Ostkirche*, Hamburg, 1957, p. 21.

86 The icon of Saint Nicholas of Mozaisk, including scenes from the Saint's life. 17th century, Zagorsk Museum.

87 *Virgin and Child with Saints*. Icon, 15th century, Zagorsk Museum.

88 *Saints Zosima and Sabbatios*. Icons, 17th century, Zagorsk Museum.

89 *Founder's Icon with Saints* (detail). 16th century, Zagorsk Museum. Old Russia's icons once displayed very bright colors, but with time the egg tempera became discolored, which is probably why many icons were eventually covered with sheets of silver and gold. As embodiments of the eternal, icons should radiate some of the magnificence of God, in the manner of the golden grounds in Byzantine mosaics.

90 *The Resurrection of Christ and His Victory over Hell*. Icon in the narthex of the Church of the Resurrection in Kinezma. 18th century.

91 *Saint Sergiy of Radonezh*. Icon, 17th century, Zagorsk Museum.

92 *Saint Sergiy of Radonezh Seeing the Virgin Mary in a Vision*. Icon, 16th century, Zagorsk Museum.

93 The Virgin Mary as Patroness of the Monastery of Pskov, which was first built in caves. Mural, executed in oil, 20th century.

94 A view across the west wall of the Pskov "Monastery of the Caves" (Pechery Lavra) onto one of the monastery churches. The Pechery Lavra was refortified the last time by Peter the Great. See also Plate 93.

95 Metropolitan John of Pskov and Pochaev celebrating the liturgy in the Church of the Assumption at the Pskov "Monastery of the Caves." Here we see the great procession into the church, during which offerings are carried from the preparatory tables through the church and onto the main altar. This part of the service becomes a symbolic laying to rest in the grave. The deacon wears the paten on his head while the priest carries the chalice.

96 *Proskomedia*, the preparation of the Eucharistic offerings of bread and wine, on the *prothesis* table in the northern part of the sanctuary.

97 The priest makes a suggestion.

98–99 The communion of the celebrants.

100, 101, 103 The monks of the Pskov "Cave Monastery" have to care for an extensive flock. Here farmers and their wives have come for the liturgy.

102 At the end of the liturgy the Metropolitan receives the choir leader.

104 The *panegia* rite after the liturgy in the Pskov Monastery. A *prosfora* with the picture of the Virgin Mary is carried in a chalice from the church into the refectory. Following the meal, pieces of the *prosfora* are divided among the brethren, in accordance with the tradition of the Apostolic Church whereby one seat at table is kept free for the Virgin Mary. The Apostles also kept one piece of bread for her, then divided it among themselves and consumed the food only after the meal.

105 After the liturgy the Metropolitan of Pskov and Pochaev blesses a sick woman at the entrance to the monastery church.

106 Following the liturgy the brethren share a meal in the refectory.

107–108 The ringing of the bells from the Pskov "Cave Monastery" announces the beginning and the end of the service. These bells are famous for their mellifluous sound, and ringing them properly is not only an art but also hard work.

109–115 The Pskov Monastery has a rule that anyone who enters an order must perform a particular service. The monks become gardeners, shoemakers, carpenters, smiths—and they even know how to repair an automobile engine. They also maintan the old tradition of baking *prosfora*.

116 The Lavra of the Assumption in Pochaev near Lvov, founded in the 13th century. Lavra is the honorary title of a major monastery.

117 Even today thousands go on pilgrimages to the many monasteries and holy places in Russia. Here the priest kneels before a wall of Pochaev Monastery and reads from the Gospels.

118 The gatekeeper, rosary in hand, sits at the entrace to the living quarters of the Pochaev Lavra.

119 A monk's cell. A monk spends many hours each day in his cell, praying before his icons. He can decorate the cell in any way he wishes.

120 The monks share a meal in the refectory of the Lavra of the Assumption in Pochaev. The monks maintain silence during meals, while one of them reads from Scripture (see the lector in the background).

121 Monks of the Monastery of the Assumption in Odessa.

122–124 Consecration of monks in the Monastery of the Assumption in Odessa. The Hegumen (head or Abbot) of the monastery tests the strength and inviolability of the monastic vows of obedience and celibacy by asking each candidate whether he voluntarily submits to monastic rule. During the act of consecration the neophyte monk's hair is symbolically shorn, and he is given a new name as a sign that he has completely forsworn the secular world and given himself wholeheartedly to the service of God. The newly consecrated monk is then handed a cross and a candle as a reminder that he has been nailed to the Cross together with Christ and has been called to serve the Savior's name in purity.

125–128 The *prosfora* bakery at the Assumption Monastery in Odessa. The *prosfora* is a round sacrificial bread made in two parts (two levels, really, as in Plate 57), which are symbolic of the two natures of Christ. Made from pure wheat flour, the *prosfora* is imprinted with the seal of the Greek cross, which has four arms of equal length separating the abbreviation of the Greek sentence *Iesous Christos nika* ("Jesus Christ is victorious"). The seal was confirmed by the Great Council of Moscow in 1667. The liturgy of the Russian Orthodox Church employs five *prosforae*. The first has the seal—representing the Lamb of God—cut out of it and is consecrated during the liturgy. The other four sacramental breads are consecrated to the memory of the Virgin Mary, to all saints, to the living, and to the dead. *Prosforae* may also, with the priest's blessing, be baked by lay members in the church community.

129 The elderly Hegumen of the Assumption Monastery in the garden.

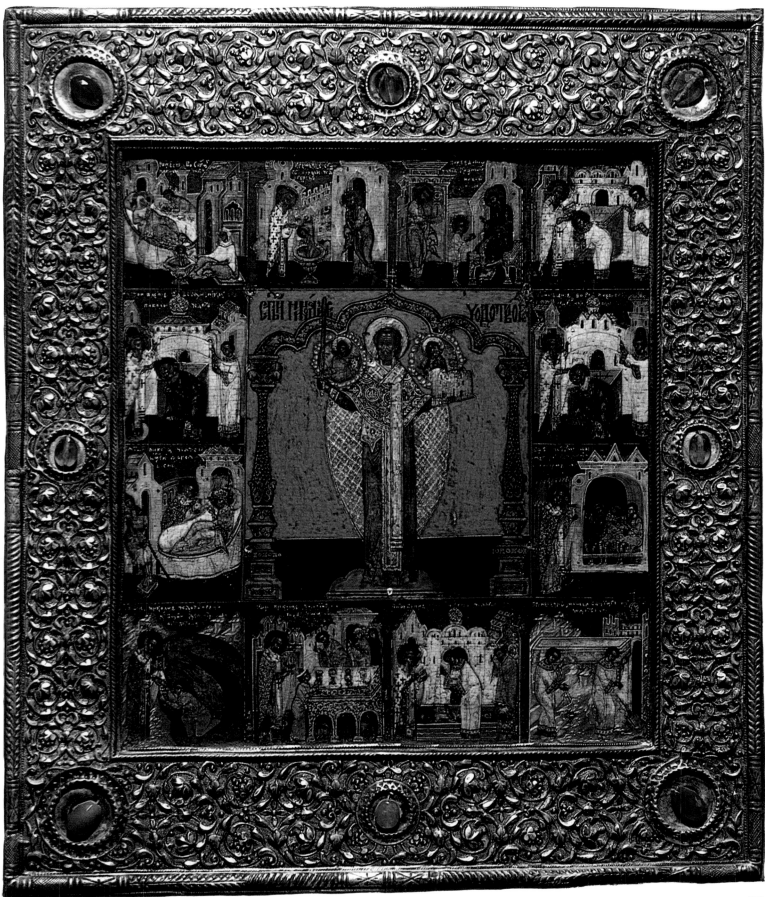

87

91

92

102

103

114

115
116▷

122

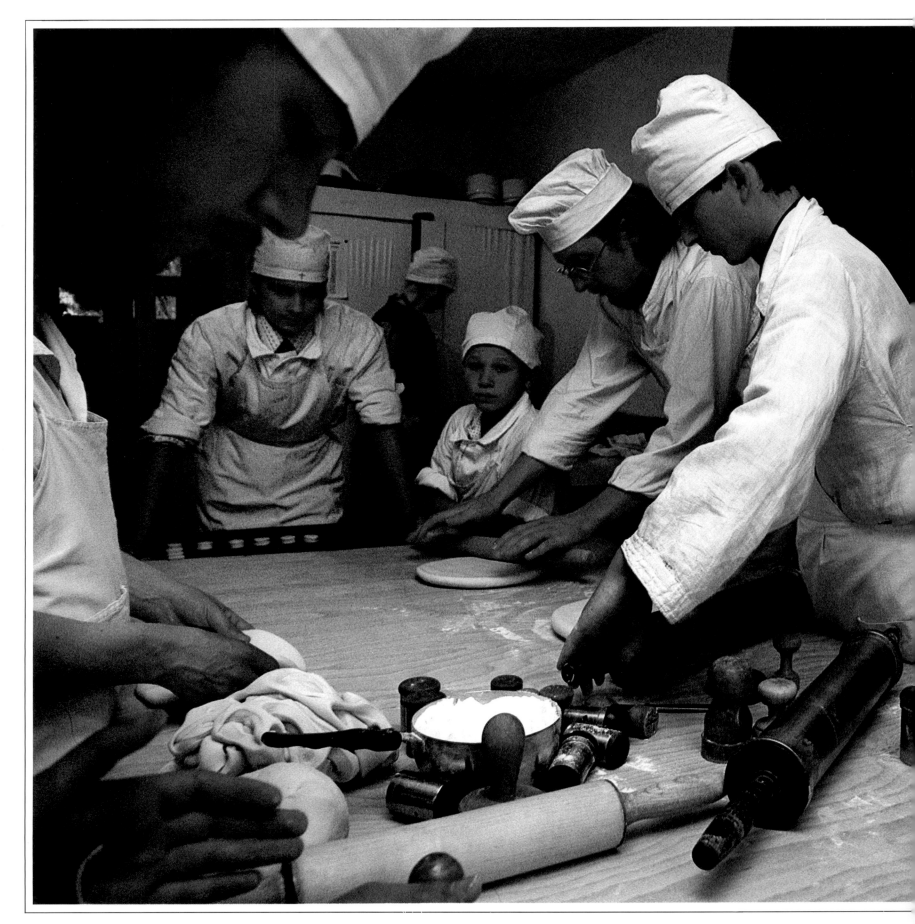

Bishop Serafim of Zurich

RUSSIAN PIETY

The center of Christian life is the liturgy. It has often been said—particularly in the Russian Orthodox Church—that ritual takes precedence over doctrine. Indeed, Russians feel that attending Divine Service is as important for the salvation of their souls as reading the Gospels, and that participating in the rites of the Church is equal to performing good deeds for the benefit of one's fellow man. The Russian nation absorbed Christianity as much from studying the *Lives of the Saints* as from studying Scripture, and received enlightenment from the veneration of shrines just as much as from listening to sermons.

Rationalists would reproach Orthodox believers for their excessive emphasis on ritual. Such a view, however, betrays a misconception of both ritual and its purpose. Just as a child's first awareness of nature predates any formal study of the world around us, ritual in the Church often introduces doctrine. Religion is not merely speculation on things divine; it must be a complete acceptance of Divinity, without reservation. Thus, for the Orthodox believer prayer welling up from the soul is infinitely important, no less so than the Eucharist—the partaking of the Body and Blood of Our Lord.

Ritual is symbolic form, reflecting the deepest spiritual content of religion, the feeling of veneration, and the devout attitude of the believer. Church ritual involves both the external, inevitably finite aspect of Christian faith *and* its enduring, innermost significance.

The great 19th-century novelist, Fyodor Dostoyevsky, explained ritual in the following manner: "They bring a vessel containing the precious fluid and everybody prostrates themselves before it, kissing and worshiping the vessel which holds the precious, life-giving fluid. Then, suddenly some worshipers get up and shout: 'You are all blind! Why kiss the vessel? Only the life-giving fluid inside is of any value, the content—not the container—is what is truly precious. Yet you kiss a piece of glass, a single piece of glass; you attribute holiness to glass, kiss it, and forget its precious content. Idol worshipers! Throw away the vessel, smash it, worship only the life-giving fluid and not a piece of glass.' And so, they smashed the vessel; its life-giving, precious fluid spilled all over the floor and was lost forever. They smashed the vessel and lost the fluid. What poor, miserable, ignorant people."

When a feeling of love overcomes us, we give it some outward expression, performing a sort of ritual, as when a mother kisses and caresses her child. The same is true in religion. If we believe in an abstract God, ritual is inappropriate; but if our God is a living and personal Presence, then the need for ritual—for a visible manifestation of our love—becomes very real.

Orthodox believers have always realized that the spirit of holiness, peace, life, and salvation permeates all their Church services, rites, and prayers. The Russian nation intuitively understands Church ritual as did Saint Basil the Great, who wrote: "Rites are religious truths derived from traditions."

But ritual also plays an important role in the exposition of doctrine. According to Archbishop

Amvrosiy of Kharkov, the Russian Orthodox Church leads us to the Redeemer through the Divine Service just as a mother leads her child by the hand. Thus, the Church and its services function like a theological school where the truths of faith and the ways of piety are learned. Merely by listening attentively to the songs and readings, writes a renowned Russian theologian, anybody who comes to Church—even without special training—can learn all he needs for the salvation of his soul. Such a school is the church with its Divine Services. And the doctrine taught at Divine Service can be grasped all the more easily because the lesson is repeated again and again throughout our lives. Moreover, Divine Services constitute practical lessons that instill the truths of faith and morality, not in some abstract form but in the very words and phrases of the prayers. By glorifying the Father, the Son, and the Holy Spirit, the supplicant can readily comprehend the doctrine of the Holy Trinity. By venerating the Cross and glorifying the Resurrection, he learns the meaning of Redemption, while grasping the dogma of the veneration of saints by actually praying to them and praising their names. So too the remembrance of the dead is understood once the acts of commemoration have been performed.

It should be noted, meanwhile, that learning from experience is not just a way of grasping the truths of faith; it is the only way. "Living religious experience is the only true way to comprehending dogma," wrote Father P. Florenskiy, the famed Russian theologian of the beginning of this century. A deep personal impulse, as well as tradition, draws the Russian people to the Church of God with its harmonious and devout services, especially those of feast days. It is said that in 19th-century Siberia escaped convicts would often be seen in church for Easter matins. So great was their attraction to the Church that they felt prepared to risk losing their freedom to attend the service.

The Orthodox Christian reverently regards the Church as the House of God, as the embodiment of a different reality—that of the Heavenly future that mankind has yet to attain and towards which humanity is ever striving.

The traditional church of Old Russia, with its white walls and gilded onion dome, seems a stern place indeed. But if the vault over a Byzantine church reminds us of the Dome of Heaven covering the earth, while the steep Gothic arch seems an expression of man's irrepressible yearning for God, then the distinctive Russian cupola, like a flame streaming toward Heaven, becomes symbolic of ardent, prayerful zeal. With its tongue of fire crowned by a cross, the Russian Orthodox church structure conveys important theological meaning. As in the Byzantine model, the interior of a Russian church represents the Universe. Overhead, inside the dome, Christ the Pantocrator blesses the world from a dark-blue sky. Under the dome, in the four corners of the church, are images of the four Evangelists, supplemented by events from their Gospels depicted on the walls. Murals at the altar represent the Heavenly Hosts and a multitude of saints. With great force, the churches of Russia create the unearthly sensation of a meeting between the divine and the human; they become a place where the world is gathered up whole and resolved into the House of God. This feeling, and the reverential attitude that the Orthodox faithful have toward their churches, comes from the fact that the Holy Rites are performed there—most especially the Eucharist, the greatest of all the sacraments—the one through which the world is united in Christ.

The prayers of the faithful said in common make the Church the vital center for Orthodox Christians. In this regard, Saint John Chrysostom, one of the most authoritative Fathers of the Orthodox Church, said in the 4th century: "Some people say we can pray in our own homes. But you deceive yourself, man! Of course, you can pray at home. But you can't pray there the way you pray in church, where such a multitude of hearts are elevated to God, uttering one common cry. Praying to the Lord all by yourself, you will not be heard as quickly as when you would pray with your brothers, because here in the church there is something far greater than you have in your room: harmony and the union of love."

"The prayer of the Russian is a spiritual phenomenon, which is little known, or completely unknown, among other nations," observed that "great prober" of Christianity, V.V. Rozanov. "This can neither be described nor expressed, you can only observe it secretly, or overhear it by chance. It consists of an awareness of one's sinfulness and unworthiness, of the complete reconciliation of the soul with those of all men, of a thirst for God's help, of hope for God's help, of faith in the miracle....Such prayer, merging with the common prayer of the whole Church, becomes suffused with the spirit of Orthodox catholicity (sobornost); it generates a special atmosphere of exaltation, compassion, sensitivity, concern for others, that universal responsiveness so glowingly described by Dostoyevsky. It is impossible not to be moved when one recalls that prayers are constantly offered up in the churches 'in all and for all' (not only for the Orthodox, and not just for our Orthodox Church), for 'the union of all' (for the well-being of all Churches of God), that God may fill men with meekness and forgiveness. People in church also pray to the Lord for the sick and 'for them who travel.' The priest prays aloud, that God may help those in the congregation 'to suppress their strife,' 'not to judge their neighbor,' 'to see their own faults,' that God may help everyone to 'dispel their sadness.' The Church prays for the fertility of the earth, 'for the peace of the whole world,' and for abundance of fruits of the earth. There is a daily prayer, beseeching God to grant the worshipers 'a Christian, peaceful end

of our life,' when the time comes. Our church service embraces everything that is trivial and all that is great in man's life in every detail, all of it absolutely understandable and highly important to us all. This accounts for the affectionate attitude of our people toward the church service. Without being aware of this affection, one simply cannot understand the Russian nation and how it came into being."[1]

It is more than just a sense of duty or reverence for the sacraments that attracts Orthodox Christians to church; they also go for the beauty of the Divine Service and the splendor of the church itself. The faithful see this beauty as the fruit of their love for the Church, whose splendor is an inspiration for the love felt by God's people.

All who write about the ritual of the Russian Orthodox Church inevitably recall the chronicle concerning Prince Vladimir's emissaries to Constantinople who were so overwhelmed by the Byzantine liturgy that they influenced the decision ultimately made by the Prince to accept Orthodox Christianity. "Nowhere on this earth is there such beauty," they related. "We did not know whether we were in Heaven or on earth." Thus, from the very beginning of Christianity in Rus, the love for the beauty present in the Divine Service has continued throughout the history of the nation's religious consciousness.

The liturgy of the Russian Church is indeed a synthesis of art forms. Beauty, like the glory of God, suffuses the church. Architecture and frescoes, icons and tapestries, the choir (which sings unaccompanied since instruments are not permitted in Orthodox churches), the poetry of hymns, the richly designed and crafted vestments, the graceful movements of the celebrants, the glow of icon lamps and candles, and the sweet

---

[1] V.V. Rozanov, *L.N. Tolstoi and the Russian Church*, St. Petersburg, 1912, pp. 14, 18.

fragrance of incense—all blend together in homage to God and beauty.

This ensemble is not merely soothing and symbolic; it is also dynamic and affective. The power of Russian churches to transform has taken a special hold over the Russian soul, a phenomenon that received such prophetic expression in the words of Dostoyevsky: "Beauty will save the world." This sensuous beauty is a manifestation of spiritual beauty, considered one of the criteria of Orthodox ecclesiasticism (tserkovnost). "What then is tserkovnost," asks Florensky, who in turn answers: "It is new life, life of the spirit. What then is the criterion of the authenticity of this new life? It is beauty. Yes, there is a special beauty which is spiritual and cannot be captured in logical formulations. Yet it is the only true way of deciding what is Orthodox and what is not.…Orthodoxy can be felt, its external appearance is recognizable, but it does not lend itself to precise definition. It is visible, but cannot be measured. Those who wish to understand Orthodoxy can only do so through immediate Orthodox experience."

It cannot be a simple thing for the layman to understand the form and content of the Orthodox liturgy. A complex interweaving of themes and prayerful recollections from various liturgical books formalized by the Church Rule, the Divine Service developed under the influence of the ancient monastic traditions of Jerusalem and Constantinople, as established in the *Typikon*.

The daily offices are set forth in two books that are part of the oldest section of the *Typikon:* the *Horologian* ("Book of Hours"), containing the fixed portions of the quotidian cycle to be used by readers and singers, and the *Sluzhebnik* ("Service Book"), which the celebrant follows. According to the Book of Hours, the following services are conducted daily: midnight service, matins, the lesser hours (prime terce, sext, and none), the liturgy, vespers, and compline. The Orthodox Church, in the tradition of the Old Testament Church, starts the liturgical day in the evening, thereby sanctifying each part of the day in prayer. First come none, vespers, and compline, at four, five, and six in our time, followed by the midnight service, matins, and prime. The daytime cycle continues with terce, sext, and the liturgy.

Each office commemorates certain particular events of sacred history. Prime commemorates the delivery of the Savior to Pilate, the false charges against Christ, and His trial; terce recalls the Descent of the Holy Spirit on the Apostles, sext the Crucifixion of Our Lord; and none His suffering and death on the Cross.

Also peculiar to the Russian Orthodox service is its sense of religious realism, characterized not only by the commemoration of events from the Gospels and Church history, but also by the very reenactment of those events in the Christian's life on earth. For example, not only is the birth of Christ celebrated in the Nativity, but the Savior is mysteriously reborn, just as He rises on Easter Sunday. The same holds true for His Transfiguration and Triumphal Entry into Jerusalem. The Church has the authority to reenact these sacred events, and the supplicants themselves become new witnesses.

Quite understandably, the ancient Monastic Rule cannot be strictly observed by today's parishioners. Parish services usually include vespers, matins, lesser hours, and the liturgy. Vespers are normally held on the eve of a feast day, and a major feast may be anticipated in an all-night vigil consisting of a joint celebration of vespers, matins, and prime. In modern times this service lasts about three hours, but if celebrated strictly according to the Rule, it would last some seven hours. And it is not customary for parishioners to sit during an Orthodox service, even during Lent when services may last five hours. Russian churches contain no pews, and standing is an ancient, ascetic tradition that helps overcome indolence and subjugate the flesh to the spirit. "When we are indolent in the service of God and prayer," said Saint Isaac Sirin, the great ascetic of the early Church, "we can see the mind begin to cloud. When the soul becomes lax in prayer, it loses the help of God, and is more likely to fall into the hands of the adversary."

On the feast day itself, terce and sext are observed, and through the liturgy the sacrament of Holy Eucharist—the very heart of the daily cycle—is celebrated. And the Church has two alternative liturgies for celebrating the Eucharist, that of Saint Chrysostom and that of Saint Basil the Great. During Lent, neither can be enacted except on Saturdays and Sundays, although on Wednesdays and Fridays the Church offers the Liturgy of the Presanctified, named by Saint Gregory the Great of Rome. At these services the faithful receive the Holy Gifts—Communion—reserved from the previous Sunday.

The Orthodox liturgy is much longer than that of the Catholic Mass; it also contains a unique first section, the *Proskomedia* ("Prothesis"). This is the setting forth of the Holy Gifts, during which bread and wine are offered. The Lamb is cut for consecration from a communion bread *(prosfora)*, while portions are removed from other loaves to honor and commemorate the Mother of God, Saint John the Baptist, the Old Testament Prophets, the Apostles Peter and Paul, and many other saints. Prayers are offered for the living and the deceased, all the while that portions of bread are cut for them as well.

Both the priest and the communicant receive the Body and Blood of Christ. And only those who have confessed prior to the liturgy are allowed to partake of the sacrament. Communicants must also observe the Eucharistic fast, which means abstaining from food and drink after the evening meal prior to Communion.

The Church also has a weekly cycle of Divine Services, a series of prayerful remembrances incorporated into services conducted on different days of the week. This cycle has existed since Apostolic times, when Christ's Resurrection was commemorated on the first day of the week. (It is interesting to note that the Russian word for Sunday is *Voskresenie* or "Resurrection." This is unparalleled in any other language, although non-Russian Christians often refer to Sunday as "the Lord's Day.") On Mondays the Divine Service offers prayers to the Heavenly Host, and on Tuesdays it is the Old Testament Prophets and, especially, Christ's forerunner, Saint John the Baptist, who are commemorated. Wednesdays and Fridays are devoted to Christ's trial, suffering, and death, with special veneration reserved for the glorious and life-giving Cross. On Thursdays the Divine Service honors the Holy Apostles, along with Saint Nicholas, the Archbishop of Myra in Lycia, the object of particular devotion in Russia. On Saturdays the Church glorifies all the saints and all those who have died in the Orthodox faith. Throughout the week the Mother of God is remembered, but most particularly on Sundays, Wednesdays, and Fridays.

The commemorative prayers of the Divine Service, all organized according to the days of the week, are fixed in the *Octoechos,* or "Book of Eight Tones," and set in eight different melodic lines, so that one tone can be used for an entire week and then replaced with another on Sunday.

The Russian Orthodox Church has evolved yet another set of liturgy, this one prepared as an annual cycle. It permits a certain saint or event in the history of human salvation to be commemorated on each day of the Church year. Always celebrated on the same days every year, these feasts are know as "immovable" or "fixed."

The cycle of movable feasts is related to that Feast of Feasts: Easter, the celebration of Christ's Resurrection. In 325 the Ecumenical Council of Nicea decreed that Easter be celebrated on the first Sunday following the full moon after or on the vernal equinox. This means that Easter may be celebrated on any Sunday falling between March 22 and April 25. And in Russia the date is further governed by the Julian calendar, which in this century lags thirteen days behind the Gregorian calendar used throughout Western Christendom. Thus, while East and West usually observe Easter on different Sundays, they do on occasion, when their calendars coincide, celebrate Christ's Resurrection on the same day—to everyone's great joy.

The Resurrection, symbolizing the triumph of life over death, is the central holiday of the Russian Orthodox Church, and the happiness created by this Feast of Feasts constitutes one of the most fundamental features of the Orthodox outlook. "For meet it is that the Heavens should rejoice, and that the earth should be glad, and that the whole world, both visible and invisible, should keep the Feast. For Christ is risen, the everlasting joy!…Now are all things filled with light: Heaven, and earth, and the places under the earth. All creation doth celebrate the Resurrection of Christ, on whom also it is founded.…We celebrate the death of Death, the annihilation of Hell, the beginning of a life new and everlasting," proclaims the Orthodox Church in the Easter Canon.

Three other movable feasts are related to Easter: that of the Lord's Entrance into Jerusalem, celebrated one week before Easter (a feast the Western Church calls Palm Sunday); our Lord's Ascension into Heaven, the celebration of which falls forty days after Easter; and, ten days after Ascension, Holy Trinity Day, or Pentecost, the Descent of the Holy Spirit on the Apostles. These three movable feasts join with nine fixed feasts to make the Twelve Great Feasts of the Orthodox Church. The nine fixed holy days of the Church year, which begins on September 1, are the following: the Nativity of the Blessed Virgin (September 8), the Exaltation of the Venerable and Life-giving Cross (September 14), the

Presentation of the Virgin in the Temple (November 21), the Nativity of Our Lord (December 25), Epiphany (January 6), the Presentation of Our Lord in the Temple (February 2), the Annunciation (March 25), the Transfiguration of Our Lord (August 6), and the Dormition of the Mother of God (August 15)— each of them preceded by an "eve" and followed by an "after-feast."

The order of services for all the fixed feasts can be found in the *Menaion,* each of whose twelve volumes is devoted to a single month. The *Pentecostarian* contains the services for the movable feasts between Easter and Pentecost. The Lenten *Triodion* provides the prayers for the ten weeks leading up to Easter, a period that begins three weeks prior to Lent and includes Lent itself and, of course, the Quadragesima or Holy Week.

Owing to the complicated nature of the system, one Divine Service may combine hymns and prayers from different cycles that happen to overlap on that date. Before all else, however, the individual service derives from the daily cycle in which the Book of Hours is used by the worshipers and the Service Book by the celebrant. Next, the *Menaion* determines whether a Saint should be commemorated or a feast from the annual cycle celebrated. The day of the week governs which commemorative prayers should be recited from the weekly cycle and which of the eight tones should be sung, the tone itself indicated by the *Octoechos.* To complicate matters still further, the liturgy for any one day may coincide with a movable feast, in which case the *Pentecostarion* or the Lenten *Triodion* must be consulted. Finally, there is the Scripture that must be read for each day, the particular passage, or lesson, chosen from one of two schedules: the Ordinary, which provides a text for each and every day, and the Festal, which indicates the readings for the various feasts. But the very complexity of the Orthodox liturgy constitutes a virtue, for the sheer wealth of ideas and feelings encompassed by the system assures that the Church has omitted nothing from the sacred history of human salvation.

Within the Divine Service, specific moments have traditionally been treated in a symbolic manner. Censing symbolizes the grace of the Holy Spirit, while the closing of the Holy Doors signifies the closing of the Gates of Paradise after the Fall. While praying both in church and in solitude, Orthodox Christians perform certain actions—such as bows and prostrations—that assume a symbolic and sacred meaning.

To cross themselves, Orthodox Christians join together their first three fingers, thereby symbolizing the Holy Trinity, while the two remaining fingers press against the palm of the hand to symbolize the Incarnation of Jesus Christ and His descent to earth as the Son of God. At the same time that they utter the sacred formula—"In the name of the Father, and of the Son, and of the Holy Spirit"—the Orthodox faithful first touch their foreheads with the first three fingers, in order to sanctify their thoughts, then touch their breasts to sanctify their hearts and feelings, and finally both their right and their left shoulders, so as to invoke the blessing of the Holy Trinity on all their labors. Altogether, the gesture from the forehead down to the chest and from the right shoulder to the left retraces the form of the Cross, which becomes an expression of faith that Christ, the Son of God, redeemed us from sin and eternal death through His Passion and Death.

The contemporary Orthodox service differs considerably from the simplicity of the early Christian service. But underneath its historical forms, the liturgy embodies the living water, the inner spontaneity of faith, the knowledge of Christ, and the Light of His Resurrection. The whole of this mystery builds to the summit of its power and expression during Holy Week. The first culminating moment of this sacred time comes on Wednesday, when the anointing of Our Lord's feet by Mary Magdalen is commemorated. Then comes Maundy Thursday, marking the institution of the Eucharist at the Last Supper. The Good Friday service is a powerful re-creation of the suffering, death, and burial of Our Lord. Now the celebrant reads the Office of the Passion, accompanied by the relevant hymns, and those in prayer seem to be standing before the Cross. In keeping with an old and pious custom, the faithful hold lighted candles during the Good Friday service and take them home afterwards. At the evening, or really afternoon, service, an image of the dead Christ—the Holy Shroud or Holy Epitaphion—is brought to the center of the church and there laid upon a tomblike elevation, an object of veneration.

The matins for Holy Saturday is the very epitome of Orthodox liturgical creativity. The service includes the Office of the Burial, which consists of special eulogies alternating with verses from Psalm 119 to unite Old Testament piety with the New Testament image of Christ descending into Hell while abiding in Heaven. The Shroud is carried around the church, as in a funeral procession. Saturday morning brings a marvelously beautiful liturgy, containing as it does the fifteen *paroemias* from the Old Testament. After they have been read, the celebrants change from their somber vestments for light-colored ones, the shift serving to announce the Resurrection, first in hymns and then in the reading of the Gospel.

On Easter Eve, the faithful gather in church before midnight to bid farewell to the Holy Shroud, as it is borne from the center of the church to the sanctuary prior to the celebration of Easter matins. At the stroke of midnight, the Holy Doors open allowing the celebrants to descend into a sea of worshipers, all holding lit candles, which add their light to the glow of candles flickering before all the icons. With bells pealing, the procession continues around the church and stops before the closed door symbolizing the sealed tomb from which the angel rolled away the stone. As the doors open the celebrants enter, singing "Christ is risen from the dead." Now the Easter matins has begun, a jubilant service suffused with divine joy. At the end of the liturgy, the celebrants and everyone else in the church kiss, saying, "Christ is risen," and responding, "He is risen indeed." After matins, the priests continue the blessing, begun on Holy Saturday, of the Easter Viands: colored eggs, *paskha* (a special cheesecake in the form of a pyramid), and *kulich* (a rich cylinder-shaped pastry with spices and raisins). For the Orthodox Christian an Easter service would be unimaginable without the procession, without the kissing, without the rites that since childhood have been associated with the Resurrection of Christ.

The same could be said for the blessing of the willow branches on Palm Sunday, the carrying of the Cross during the Veneration of the Cross week, the blessing of the apples on the Feast of the Transfiguration, the blessing of the waters on the eve of Epiphany, as well as on the feast day of Epiphany. These are not simply rites; they are the indispensable elements of Orthodox worship, the vehicles of Divine Grace.

In addition to church services and personal prayer, there are private offices for the Orthodox to perform. These include, first and foremost, the sacraments of Baptism, Marriage, and Anointing of the Sick, but also prayers offered for personal intentions, such as those for the sick, for travelers, for thanksgiving, and so forth. The *panikhidas* are offices for the dead, for the repose of their souls. For the departed, the Church also reserves special days of remembrance.

In addition to Lent, with its movable boundaries, the Orthodox Church observes three other long fasts: the Christmas Fast (November 15–December 24), the Dormition Fast (August 1–15), and Peter's Fast, which begins a week after Pentecost and ends on the Feast of the Holy Apostles Peter and Paul. Since the beginning of this fast depends on a movable feast, its length can vary from year to year. The Orthodox also fast on Wednesdays and Fridays, except during certain feast weeks. And they keep strict fasts on Christmas Eve, on the eve of the Epiphany, on the day of the Beheading of John the Baptist, and on the Feast of the Exaltation of the Cross. Should a fast day fall on certain feast days, the Rule allows for some relaxation. For example, if the eve of the Nativity or Epiphany falls on a Saturday or Sunday, food may be taken with vegetable oil, while on Wednesdays and Fridays, from Easter to Holy Trinity, fish may be eaten. Otherwise, strict fast means that even vegetable oil, along with meat, fish, and dairy products, must be foregone.

The Russian Orthodox faithful regard fasting with great reverence. Of course, there is a certain amount of relaxation, such as that just mentioned; and still it should be remembered that the rules originated with the monks of Palestine, which makes it difficult for them to be observed by modern laymen. But despite their strict attitude toward fasting, Russians have always condemned any formal observance of fasts. Fasting has never been obligatory for the sick. For most people, fasting means abstention from entertainment, more time spent in prayer, increased attendance at church, visits to the sick, and acts of mercy and love.

The Russian Church reserves more than two hundred days a year for fasting, since the denial of the body cannot be separated from the purification of the spirit. Through the grace of prayer, through acts of humility and charity, all illuminated with the love of God and of one's fellow man, the heart is cleansed of impure thoughts, feelings, and habits. During the first days of Lent the Orthodox Church sings: "We fast with a fast pleasant and well-pleasing unto the Lord, for the true fast is shunning all evil, checking one's tongue, avoiding wrath, and removing oneself from lust, from lies, from perjury. The estrangement from these is the true and well-pleasing fast." During a fast, church services become longer, in the course of which numerous prostrations are prescribed, and the whole atmosphere inside the church changes. The clergy wear dark vestments, icons are draped with black cloth, and hymns take on a sorrowful and penitential tone. During each daily service, the priest recites the prayer of Saint Ephraim the Syrian, while the faithful echo him, making four prostrations and twelve bows from the waist and praying: "O Lord and Master of my life, grant not unto me a spirit of slothfulness, of discouragement, of lust for power, of vain babbling [reverence]. But vouchsafe unto me, thy servant, the spirit of continence, of meekness, of patience, and of love [reverence]. Yea, O Lord and King, grant that I may percieve my own transgressions, and judge not any brother. For blessed art thou unto ages of ages. Amen [reverence]."

A fast is an ideal time for *eulavation,* a pious Orthodox custom consisting of personal preparation for receiving Holy Communion throughout an entire week. In addition to fasting, both physical and spiritual, the devout Orthodox Christian attends church regularly, venerates shrines, recites all the designated prayers, and reads Scripture and other sacred texts. The behavior is that of one preparing to face God. Seclusion, being conducive to self-examination, should be sought as frequently as possible. Before receiving the Holy Gifts, the believer goes to confession and enters into the sacrament of Penance.

Most practicing Orthodox Russians go through eulavation once a year, during Lent, but they also take Holy Communion more often,

usually during the long fasts and one's Name Day (the feast of one's Patron Saint). Naturally, there is nothing to prevent more frequent eulavation, or even continuing the practice all the time.

The Eucharist constitutes the focal point of the entire life of Christ's Church. It combines the great and mysterious sacrifice of Golgotha (with its expression of God's infinite love), the unification of the Church Triumphant and the Church Militant in reverential and grateful admiration for the greatness of this mystery, and the common prayer for both the living and the departed members of the Church. The Eucharist, by which every Christian partakes of the divine, everlasting life, is the focal point in the personal, spiritual being of every practicing Orthodox Christian. Receiving the Holy Mysteries of Christ forms the very foundation of Christian existence; thus, in the absence of Holy Communion, the spiritual life of the Orthodox becomes impossible.

During the past decade there has been a growing desire among the faithful in many Russian Orthodox parishes to communicate more often. But inevitably this zeal has been restrained by age-old disciplinary requirements and the special reverence felt for the Mystery of the Eucharist, along with the fear this engenders of approaching the Body and Blood of Christ unworthily. Fortunately, the Orthodox liturgy gives the layman an opportunity to participate in the Eucharistic Supper without actually partaking of the Holy Gifts. This can be done through reverential presence at the Mystery of the Divine Service, which means sharing in it, and then by partaking of the Eucharistic or Communion bread. The bread from which the particle is taken for immersion in the Holy Chalice is the material sign of spiritual communion, as is the *Antidoron,* which, being the remains of the loaves offered in the setting forth of the Holy Gifts, is a "substitute" for those Gifts. Moreover, there is the Church's tradition of the *agapy* (from the Greek *agape,* meaning "love"), which in the beginning was closely associated with the Eucharist. Agapy allows those particles removed from oblations for the living and the departed to be taken home by the faithful, who reverently consume them before meals.

For the Orthodox Christian there is nothing more important than the Eucharist. Still, the faithful acknowledge the beneficent effect of the prayers said and the hymns sung in church, of candles lit before icons, which are not mere gestures and symbols, but religious rites—that is, actions or formulas that, although resembling ordinary words and actions, differ from them in that they possess a mysterious, mystical, supernatural force.

Clearly, the daily life of the Orthodox Christian differs from that of a nonreligious person. It is no coincidence that Russia has the old proverb: "Without God, you couldn't reach the threshold." In the pious Orthodox family, prayer invariably precedes meals, sleep, and tasks, and every work day concludes with thanksgiving. In the absence of prayers, the faithful make the sign of the Cross. As in Old Russia, homes display icons, always hung on the wall in places of honor. In this way the Orthodox family observes the admonition of the *Domostroi*: "The house should be decorated with holy images and kept clean. In every Christian's home there should be holy images throughout every chamber, properly placed on the walls and grandly decorated, with candles in front of every image, lit at times of prayer and then extinguished, with a curtain covering the image for the sake of cleanliness and neatness and for preservation....It is like a temple to be kept clean, the holy images treated with reverence, with a clear conscience, and at times of prayer to God [you should] always venerate them, even with tears and crying and with a contrite heart to implore the forgiveness of sins."

The basic feature of Russian piety is its striving towards sanctity in concrete, tangible form. Thus, the Orthodox faithful like to touch holy objects, kiss them, and wear them close to their hearts, and to sanctify their homes with them. The iconoclasts tried to deprive Orthodoxy of these sacred shrines, but were defeated, and the victory over the desecrators of shrines was so joyful that the Russian Orthodox Church commemorates it in the Office of the Triumph of Orthodoxy, the liturgy read during the first Sunday in Lent.

Present within the life view and religious fervor evinced by the children of Russian Orthodoxy is a remarkable integrity, a wholeness rooted in a profound understanding of the significance of absolute spiritual values, an abiding sense of the transfiguration of the world. A unique spiritual tradition, it has sanctified the life of the Russian nation, and today it suffuses every manifestation of religious life: the Divine Service, prayer, icon veneration, the cult of the saints, works of charity, and the tradition of *startsy*, or spiritual guidance sought from one's elders. Russian Orthodoxy would be unthinkable without this heritage, which can, perhaps, be defined simply as "piety," expressed in prayer, works of charity, and fasting. To the Russian Orthodox believer, these are the means by which the Christian receives the Holy Spirit, the true goal of all Christian life.

130 Mural in the Resurrection Monastery of Saint Florov in Kiev. This monastery, which dates back to 1566, commemorates in a special way the great Russian priest of the 19th century, Saint Serafim of Sarov. The folklike naïveté of the painting, which shows the Saint in the forest, has an affinity with the painting of France's Douanier Rousseau, a near contemporary of the Russia's Saint Serafim.

131 A workday in the Convent of the Resurrection Church of Saint Florov in Kiev.

132 Supervised by the younger Abbess, the old caretaker carefully manages the household at the Resurrection Convent in Florov.

133 Sisters of the Convent of the Assumption at Piukhtitsy on their way to the evening service in the Church of the Assumption. Novices in their peaked caps lead the way.

134 Abbess Varvara of the Convent of the Assumption in Piukhtitsy during a liturgy.

135 Nuns and novices during a service.

136 A nun praying in church.

137 Psalmody.

138–139 Nuns and lay worshipers at evening prayer.

140 Caring for elderly and ill sisters is an honorable duty for nuns and novices. Here the oldest sister in the convent—101 years of age and wearing the habit of the Great Schema (the strictest form of Eastern monasticism)—is supported by two nuns.

141 The flower garden of Piukhtitsy Convent.

142 Abbess Varvara in conversation with two farmers' wives who have sought her out after the service to ask for advice and consolation.

143 Nuns and novices of the Assumption Convent in Piukhtitsy. The director of the convent choir, Mother Georgia, stands to the right of Abbess Varvara.

144 The convent church is always decorated with flowers. They stand before the church's revered icons, which are thought to perform miracles, before the feast-day icons, and in front of the *Epitaphion*, the cloth with the Entombment of Christ represented on it. Nuns especially love white flowers for their purity.

145 Piukhtitsy Convent is also a large and well-organized farm where the sisters do the work themselves. Here a group of them return from mowing hay.

146–150 Picking berries and mushrooms in the vast forests surrounding the convent is an important summer and fall activity. The berries are made into jams and the mushrooms dried and salted down; eventually they all help to enrich the meager convent fare.

151–152 The Piukhtitsy Convent has been keeping bees for centuries. Note the tiny replica of the convent church among the beehives.

153–155 The nuns of Piukhtitsy at their everyday tasks in the kitchen, in the shed, and at washing in the open.

156 Knitting *paraments* is an important source of income for the Piukhtitsy Convent.

157 Novices set the table in the refectory.

158–159 Some of the nuns are excellent tailors, seamstresses, and embroiderers. The vestments worn by Bishops are generally produced in convents. In Plate 159 a Bishop's crown is being prepared.

160 The Convent of Piukhtitsy buys its grain in the neighboring collective but bakes the bread itself. The product is famous not only for its size, but also for its taste and the unusually long duration of its freshness.

161 Although Piukhtitsy has had its own boiler and steam heat for some time, the cells and some of the other convent rooms are still heated with wood in the old way. Here the nuns split and saw wood prior to building it into large beehive-shaped stacks.

162 Each sister has her own cell, which is modestly furnished with table, chair, and bed. An absolute must, however, is the house icon before which every sister recites her various daily prayers.

134
◁133

143
144▷
145▷▷

146

147

149

148

150

162

V. Feodorov

THE CONTEMPORARY LIFE OF THE RUSSIAN ORTHODOX CHURCH

No account of the present-day life of the Russian Orthodox Church, a Church whose history goes back a thousand years and whose flock numbers in the millions, would be complete without a description of its structure and administration, its theological schools and parish activity, its relationship to the state, and its various commitments: patriotic, peace-making, and ecumenical. We should also describe the faithful and mention both those who stand upon the threshold of the Church and those who remain outside the walls.

Within the diptych (the traditional hierarchical system) of the local Orthodox Churches, the Russian Church occupies the fifth position, behind the Churches of Constantinople, Alexandria, Antioch, and Jerusalem but ahead of the Churches of Georgia, Serbia, Rumania, Bulgaria, Cyprus, and Hellas, the Orthodox Churches of Poland and Czechoslovakia, the Autocephalus Orthodox Church in America, and the Autonomous Churches of Sinai, Finland, and Japan.

Like other Orthodox Churches, the Russian Church is governed structurally and administratively by the Canon Law, which consists of the Apostolic Canons, decrees of the Ecumenical and Local Councils, and the rules of the Holy Fathers, all inherited from the Early Universal Church. In matters of dogma, Church administration, and ecclesiastical law, the supreme authority is exercised legislatively, administratively, and juridically by the Local Council of the Russian Orthodox Church, which meets periodically and is composed of bishops, clergymen, and laymen.

In accordance with the 34th Canon of the Holy Apostles, the leader of the Russian Church is His Holiness the Patriarch of Moscow and All Russia. Invested with the power to address the entire Russian Church on ecclesiastical matters, the Patriarch maintains contact with the Primates of all the other Local Churches. His Holiness can call meetings of the whole Church hierarchy, and for major questions of ecclesiastical policy, he can summon the Local Council of the Russian Orthodox Church. Issues that must be coordinated with the Soviet government are handled by the Patriarch through the Council for Religious Affairs, which functions under the auspices of the USSR Council of Ministers. His Holiness bestows awards for outstanding achievement in the field of religion, and his name is cited at every Divine Service in all Russian Orthodox Churches throughout the world. When the Patriarchal seat is vacant, the duties of His Holiness fall to the Patriarchal Yoeum Tenens, who is the senior permanent member of the Holy Synod until a Local Council meets to elect a new leader. The Patriarch of Moscow and All Russia since 1971 is His Holiness Pimin (Izvekov), formerly the Metropolitan of Krutitsky and Kolmna and Yoeum Tenens of the Patriarchal See.

The Patriarch governs the Russian Church together with the Holy Synod, of which His Holiness is chairman and which includes the following permanent members: the Metropolitans of Kiev and Galich (Patriarchal Exarchate to the Ukraine), Leningrad and Novgorod, Krutitsky and Kolomna (the title of the Metropolitan of the Moscow diocese) and the head of the Department of External Church Relations and the Chancellor of the Moscow Patriarchate. In addition to its permanent members, the Synod summons by turns three members from among the diocesan hierarchs to attend the regular sessions of the Synod, which meets every six months. The decisions taken there are carried out through the Chancellery of His Holiness the Patriarch, which presently is headed by His Eminence Metropolitan Aleksiy of Tallinn and Estonia and Chancellor of the Moscow Patriarchate.

In 1946 the Holy Synod established the Department of External Church Relations, which maintains relations with institutions of the Russian Orthodox Church abroad, other Local Orthodox Churches, non-Orthodox Churches and religious associations, ecumenical organizations, and institutions of non-Christian religions, as well as with international public and governmental organizations concerned with preserving and consolidating world peace. The present head of this department is His Eminence Metropolitan Filaret of Minsk and Belorussia, who succeeds the world-renowned ecumenical figure Metropolitan Nikodim of Leningrad and Novgorod, who before his death in 1978 had been President of the World Council of Churches and the Honorary President of the Christian Peace Conference. For many years Metropolitan Nikodim was Chairman of the Holy Synod Commission on Christian Unity and Inter-Church Relations. Today the chairman of this body is Metropolitan Filaret of Kiev and Galich.

The Holy Synod Commission on Christian Unity and Inter-Church Relations coordinates the participation of the Russian Orthodox Church in Pan-Orthodox theological activities and in theological dialogues with non-Orthodox confessions, and it submits recommendations to the Holy Synod in matters concerning the theological aspects of the ecumenical movement. The commission includes twenty-four theologians, hierarchs, clergymen, and laymen.

The Holy Synod also administers the Publishing Department, the Education Committee, the Development of Economic Management, and the Pension Committee.

Since 1943 the Russian Orthodox Church has issued a monthly publication entitled *The Journal of the Moscow Patriarchate*, which in 1971 became available in English. In 1945 the Publishing Department of the Moscow Patriarchate came into being. It now functions under the directorship of His Grace Archbishop Pitirim of Volokolamsk, who is also editor-in-chief of the journal. The Publishing Department puts out service books, periodicals, and, since 1959, a series entitled *Theological Studies*, which contain articles by contemporary theologians and some of the best unpublished works from the past. Publications in recent years include a fourth edition of the Bible in Russian and three editions of the New Testament, along with a sequence of service books.

The Education Committee, headed by His Eminence Metropolitan Aleksiy of Tallinn and Estonia, has jurisdiction over the theological schools, approving their curricula and dealing with all problems related to religious education and training.

The Department of Economic Management, established in 1946 and now headed by Protopresbyter M.H. Stadnyuk, sees to the practical needs of the parishes, supervising the workshops that produce candles, icons, sacred vessels, liturgical vestments, incense, and other items required in religious observance. It also assists in the repair and restoration of churches, monasteries, and other structures belonging to the Church. In 1980 the department opened a workshop outside Moscow.

The Pension Committee, created in 1948 and run by Archpriest D.A. Akinfiev, examines applications for grants and pensions submitted with the recommendation of the diocesan hierarchs. The applications concern retired workers and employees of church organizations and institutions, as well as nonworking members of their families whose breadwinner has died. For the purpose of increasing the pensions, the "Enactment on Pensions and Allowances to the Clergy of the Russian Orthodox Church" was revised in 1957 and 1970. The pensions and grants are paid from the fund of the Moscow Patriarchate, the fund accruing from annual contributions made by the diocesan administrations as well as from pension funds that are in turn made up of taxes collected on the incomes of parishes and their clergy.

For purposes of administration, the Russian Orthodox Church is divided into dioceses. In keeping with an age-old practice, diocesan borders correspond to those of the state administrations—that is, according to district, region, and republic. Also in keeping with tradition, each diocese bears the name of its cathedral city, which is the administrative center of the district, region, or republic. In a few instances, two or more such units are joined into one diocese for reasons of territory, demography, or confession. In Siberia, for instance, the density of population is much lower than in the European part of the Soviet Union, and in some areas the adherents to other confessions outnumber the Orthodox, as do the Catholics of Lithuania and the Muslims of Tadzhikistan or Uzbekistan. Moreover, the number of parishes in each diocese varies from region to region.

At the present time the Russian Orthodox Church comprises 76 dioceses, some of which are combined into exarchates, as in the Ukraine, in Western and Central Europe, and in Central and South America. Some foreign parishes of the Russian Church come under the aegis of deaneries, which can be found both in Hungary and Finland. The Moscow Patriarchate deals directly with a number of parishes in the United States, Canada, and Morocco, and representatives of the Patriarch are attached to parishes in Alexandria, Damascus, Beirut, Belgrad, Karlovy Vary, New York, and Tokyo. And the Russian Orthodox Mission has long been present in Jerusalem.

The Holy Synod nominates Bishops, designates their see, and rules on their transfer from one see to another. According to the canons of the Orthodox Church, a Bishop must be a monk; he cannot be chosen from among secular priests or celibates attached to a monastery. Once nominated, he is consecrated by at least two hierarchs. A successor to the Apostles, a prime teacher of the faith, a preacher of Christian truths, the Bishop is invested with a plenitude of ecclesiastical power. He supervises diocesan hierarchs, administers chancelleries and monasteries that fall within his see, and oversees the church workshops. The Bishop ordains priests and deacons for his diocese, appoints deans, rectors, and other clerics. In larger dioceses, vicars are appointed to assist the Bishops. Traditionally, vicars of the Moscow diocese are sent to institutions abroad; for example, Bishop Irenei of Serpukhov is the administrator of the Patriarch's parishes in the United States and Canada, while Bishop Valentin of Zvenigorod represents the Moscow Patriarchate at the Patriarchate of Antioch.

The diocesan hierarch, or Bishop, can gather experienced clerics into a council to assist him in the execution of his duties. For the sake of convenience, moreover, a diocese may be divided into deaneries headed by superintendent deans who visit parishes, supervise the clergy, and transmit instructions from the Bishop. If necessary, they give fraternal guidance to the rectors of parishes, make certain that the religious needs of the faithful are satisfied, and recommend various members of the clergy for special award.

How does the Russian Orthodox Church train new clerics? Primarily through theological schools, and today the Russian Church maintains three seminaries and two religious academies. The Moscow Theological Academy and Seminary are located near the capital, on the grounds of the Trinity–Saint Sergiy Lavra at Zagorsk. Founded in the 14th century by Saint Sergiy of Radonezh, this institution occupies a prominent place in Russian history. These schools were reopened in 1944, those of Leningrad in 1946, and the Odessa Seminary was brought back in 1945. They all carry on the finest traditions of the past. A number of instructors who were either teachers or graduates of the prerevolutionary theological schools now provide a living link to the past. For example, Archpriest Professor Mikhail Speransky, a graduate of the St. Petersburg Theological Academy, heads the faculty for New Testament studies at what is now the Leningrad Theological Academy.

The seminaries and academies of the Russian Orthodox Church have trained several thousand priests. Of these, approximately 1,000 have the equivalent of a Bachelor's Degree in Theology, 60 are Masters of Theology, 15 have completed doctorates in theology. But statistics are merely indicative. In his speech to the annual convocation of Moscow's theological schools in 1979, Patriarch Pimin said: "Many are seeking the well of [living] water springing up into everlasting life [John 4:14]. And this imposes an obligation on our theological schools; the education received by students should be evaluated not so much by scholarly titles as by the implementation of Christ's teaching in the life of our graduates who become pastors or monks, teachers of theology and ecumenical leaders, ecclesiastical historians and writers."

The principal task of theological schools is to train clergymen capable of awakening moral force in men, the better to foster the consolidation and continuation of the Church. What makes the schools unique is that, besides providing

specialized education, they prepare pastors, in the words of Saint Paul, "to be an example to the believers in word, in conversation, in charity, in spirit, in faith, in purity" (I Timothy 4:12). This is the principle that guides the theological seminaries and academies of present-day Russian Orthodoxy, since the Church's ministry is to perpetuate the work of salvation begun by Our Lord Jesus Christ, who came to "save that which was lost" (Matthew 18:11).

The theological seminaries are, in fact, specialized secondary schools, open to anyone between 18 and 35 years of age who wishes to serve the Church. An entrance examination is required, in addition to a letter of recommendation from either a parish priest or diocesan hierarch. After taking the examination in the Russian language, the candidate must write an essay on a theme from the Gospel, after which he is interviewed: The most worthy and best-prepared candidates are then selected for admission. In the past six years, enrollment has doubled, but still many applicants must be turned down.

Those accepted can look forward to four years of study, during which they will live together as one large family, sharing a disciplined life that is almost monastic. The students, like the seminary, are supported totally by the Church, and they attend classes every day except Sundays and holidays, taking courses in general theology, liturgy, history, and modern languages. Early on they study the history of both the Old and the New Testaments, catechism, the Church Rule, general Church history, history of the Russian Church, and the Church Slavonic used in Divine Services and singing. In their third and fourth years, seminarians pursue more advanced studies in the Old and New Testaments, dogmatic and ethical theology, apologetics, comparative theology, and homiletics. They also learn to deal with the everyday, practical problems of a parish priest and take courses on the beliefs of various sects, as well as on the Constitution and history of the Soviet Union. They study both Greek and Latin and must master a modern language of their own choice.

During a six-month term seminarians write two essays on topics proposed by department heads, and at term's end they take examinations in all their courses. They have the run of the seminary libraries, some of which are extremely rich, like the library of the Leningrad theological schools, which has about 200,000 books, or that in Moscow, which has close to 300,000 volumes. And, of course, they have access to the state public libraries as well.

Upon graduation, some students are appointed to various dioceses and many of the appointees have already taken Holy Orders. Meanwhile, the top third of the class go on to another four years of study at the academy. Here, they go deeper into the subjects learned in the seminary and take new studies in patrology, ecclesiastical law, Early Church history, Church archaeology, Byzantium, history of the Slavic Churches, Western faiths, non-Chalcedonian Churches, logic, and stylistics.

In both seminary and academy, the training and lessons center on the Church service. Every student attends his school's church for morning and evening prayers, for Divine Liturgy on Sundays and feast days, and he maintains the All-Night Vigil on the eve of feasts. Before classes in the morning and after lessons in the evening, the seminarians conduct services, those in Holy Orders alternating as priests and deacons, those who are not, as readers, choristers, and sacristans. The place of worship is of paramount importance in an institution devoted to the formation of future clerics who will be called upon to develop the Orthodox tradition of leading the flock.

During their vacations, seminarians gain practical experience in parishes or monasteries, and at the end of the academic year every class makes a pilgrimage to one of the dioceses. Once they have completed their course of study, the more gifted students defend a thesis to obtain the degree of Candidate of Theology, and the very best receive a scholarship, permitting them to remain in the academy. Within a year or two, they join the faculty of either the seminary or the academy.

For the sake of further study in a variety of specialized areas, as well as for the benefit of deeper ecumenical experience, the Russian Church sends certain young theologians abroad to Orthodox as well as to Catholic and Protestant educational institutions for a period of two or three years. In recent times, students from both the Moscow and the Leningrad Theological Academies have studied at the Faculty of Theology of Athens University, the Eastern Institute in Rome, the Catholic Institute of Paris, the Department of Catholic Theology of the University of Regensburg in the Federal Republic of Germany, and the Ecumenical Institute at Bosse, Switzerland.

Graduates of the Moscow Theological Academy may take a three-year postgraduate course, and those who complete it either participate in the ecumenical activities of the Orthodox Church or return to their parishes.

In 1969, all three theological schools opened precentorial courses in which musically gifted students learn, in addition to their other subjects, to direct church choirs. This, however, did not solve the problem of forming a sufficient number of precentors, since most students in these courses ultimately become priests. In 1979, following a decision of the Synod, the Leningrad Theological Academy began opening the courses for precentors to young lay persons, most of whom are women. The nonseminarians also receive a theological education and ecclesiastical training.

Before the Revolution, most students in the seminaries were children of priests and other members of the clergy. Consequently, the choice of a religious education was often more a matter of family tradition than a true calling, and the graduates of the theological academies were far from unanimous in their career choice. In certain seminaries, only a quarter of the graduates took up a religious career, while the rest chose secular professions, and many people in Holy Orders were not distinguished by their religious fervor. All this reflects the fact that, in Imperial Russia, the Church was a state institution. Such is no longer the case, and children of the clergy have a wide choice of schools for higher education available to them. The majority of seminary graduates who enter Holy Orders today do so by conscious decision. Some who enter the seminary have just recently been baptized; other young men received baptism in infancy but grew up without religious instruction and have returned to the Church in their maturity. Of course, a large number of young people in the seminary come from religious families and for them the choice of vocation is a natural continuation of childhood experience. Those who have recently entered the church, or those who have returned to it, are generally no less fervent in their faith than the seminarians with a lifetime of religious experience. Many students are around thirty years of age. And most have already fulfilled their military service; those who have not interrupt their studies for two or three years in order to meet this obligation.

Every year the seminaries increase their admissions of school and college graduates who have worked in other fields for a few years. A growing number of mathematicians, physicists, doctors, lawyers, biologists, engineers, and philologists are now lecturers and professors in the Russian Orthodox theological schools and academies. They have all taken Holy Orders, and about half of them also take monastic vows,

further evincing the carefully thought out and deliberated nature of their calling.

In addition to Soviet citizens, the theological schools admit students from twenty different countries, including Bulgaria, Hungary, Greece, the United States, France, Ethiopia, and Japan. Some also come from the foreign parishes of the Moscow Patriarchate; others from different Orthodox and non-Chalcedonian Churches of the East.

To a large extent, the future of the Church will be determined by the training given in theological schools to those who presently have a calling to become pastors. In the words of Saint Basil the Great, a pastor must be "an adornment of the Church, a support of the Motherland, a pillar and ground of truth, a stronghold of faith in Christ, a strong defender of his own, an invincible force against the enemy, and a guardian of the Holy Father's decrees." He must not stand apart from the social and cultural life of his people and flock, and in this age of scientific and technological revolution, he must strive to acquire a well-rounded and thorough education. In the past, the clergy of the Orthodox Church and other Christian faiths were subject to reproach for their avoidance of social problems and issues. Today, nobody can say that the future pastors of the Russian Church are sheltered from the intense social and cultural life of their nation. No young man feels isolated from society in a Russian Orthodox seminary.

The intense nature of the seminary program does not leave time for study of mathematics and physics, as was the case in the 19th century. But secular specialists give general lectures on astronomy, biology, psychology, literature, and legal affairs, and students attend concerts, go to the theater and museums, and tour the historical and cultural places of the Soviet Union.

The theological schools take an active part in inter-Orthodox activities and the ecumenical movement. Theological and ecclesiastical conferences take place in their halls and with their participation. All seminaries and academies of the Russian Church belong to the Syndesmos, a world fellowship of Orthodox youth organizations, and the theological schools also participate in the Ecumenical Youth Council in Europe.

It is a tradition of the Russian Orthodox Church that Bishops may ordain pious laymen even if they have not been educated in the seminary. Such candidates are usually trained as sextons or readers in parish churches, and after ordination they take correspondence courses from the Moscow Theological Seminary. At the present time some nine hundred priests are enrolled in these courses.

There is no such thing as a typical day in the life of a Russian Orthodox parish. In large cities, a parish may minister to thousands of believers, whereas in the rural areas the Sunday liturgy may draw no more than five and ten souls. The parish is the nucleus of life within the Russian Church, and it is generally made up of believers who regularly attend that particular parish. In certain cases, where the congregation constitutes a well-defined community whose members all know one another personally, one can speak of a communal parish life. And this is generally the case in small towns or villages with only one church. Elsewhere, particularly in large cities, people come from different neighborhoods and often have little opportunity to become acquainted. Some believers attend a number of different churches and confess to several priests, their choice depending either on proximity or preference for a particular priest as spiritual guide.

The present-day legal status of the Church parish in the Soviet Union is based on a decree of January 23, 1918, entitled "On the Separation of the Church from the State, and Schools from the Church." This characterizes religious associations that, as private groups, may not benefit from the privileges of the state and cannot be subsidized by its autonomous and self-governing bodies. The Church's legal status was further defined in a resolution of April 8, 1929, taken by the All-Russia Central Executive Committee and the Council of the People's Commissars of the RSFSR and entitled "On Religious Associations." It specifies that believers who form a religious association may freely use a house of worship and hold meetings on other premises, providing these are leased under a contract with the authorized representatives of the local authorities. A number of new churches have recently been built in the Novgorod region, at Novokuznetsk and Vladivostok, and in the Altai. Houses of worship have also been opened in dozens of newly constructed Siberian towns.

For purposes of management, including the use of Church property, religious communities elect an executive council consisting of three parishioners. This council maintains the church, furnishes its practical needs, takes care of repairs, heating, and lighting, and supplies the materials needed for Divine Service, such as vestments, candles, and prayer books. The council also administers parish finances, accounting for its income and expenditures. Church income is derived from voluntary contributions made by the congregation and other private groups. These funds pay the clergy on a monthly basis, cover parish expenses, including major repairs, and make the parish's contribution to the diocesan administration, which in turn finances the theological schools, the Department of External Church Relations, etc.

The parish priest commands considerable respect, looked to by the parishioners not only as a spiritual leader and father figure, but also as an advisor on daily problems. Orthodox believers follow the ancient tradition of asking their priest's blessing before embarking on any major undertaking. The ministry of the priest as the shepherd of souls has always been a lofty responsibility, but today the importance of the clergyman's personality has increased many times over. Parish life, moreover, varies greatly, depending on the character of the pastor. Believers from within and from without the parish are attracted to a priest of high moral principles, dedicated to his flock, a priest whose sermons are inspired and erudite, who officiates in a lofty, disciplined manner and in strict accordance with Rule, who during confession is attentive and ready to help his parishioners.

Monasticism based on voluntary vows of chastity, obedience, and poverty has always played an especially important role in the Russian Orthodox Church. Monks and nuns are constantly offering prayers for every person in the world as well as for the world as a whole, and a complete round of daily service is observed in every cloister. Aside from communal prayer and observance of the monastic Rule, monks and nuns must carry out such tasks as baking the communion bread, working in the kitchen, making liturgical vestments, gardening, painting icons, and so forth. A number of monks are also drafted to serve as parish priests.

At the present time, there are six monasteries and twelve convents in the Russian Orthodox Church. The Moscow Patriarchate also has jurisdiction over the Gorneu Convent near Jerusalem, and the Russian Church sends monks to the Saint Panteleimon Monastery on Mount Athos, which, like all Greek monasteries, is administered by the Patriarch of Constantinople. Founded in the 11th century, this monastery was given in perpetuity to Russian monks by the Athos Council of Elders in the 12th century. However, as with other non-Greek monasteries on Mount Athos, the restriction on entry of non-Greek monks to the Saint Panteleimon Monastery has caused substantial difficulties and a significant decline in the population.

The Orthodox Church is a family of fully equal and equally honored Local Churches, whose spiritual community rests on a common point of view concerning the Eucharist and the liturgical life, as well as on a common zeal in the preservation of the treasures of Orthodoxy. The underlying principle of their relations may be expressed thus: "In most important matters, unity; in questions of secondary importance, freedom; in everything, love."

The ecumenical activities of the Russian Orthodox Church are one of the most significant features of its contemporary life. The Church believes it possible to appraise and accept the spiritual values of other Churches without betraying its own spiritual treasures. For the Orthodox Church, ecumenism is unthinkable without the Christian love that brings mutual enrichment irrespective of differences of belief.

The history of the Russian Church abounds in manifestations of the true spirit of ecumenism. In the 11th century, following the Great Schism, the Russian and Catholic Churches exchanged messages, and the Russian Church has made many assessments of inter-Christian relations as well as pronouncements through such Church hierarchs as Metropolitan Platon (Gorodetsky) of Kiev (1803–91), who said: "Our earthly fences do not reach up to Heaven."

During World War II, the Russian Church became especially conscious of the need to pray for every human soul requiring God's help and grace. His Holiness Patriarch Sergiy gave his blessing to special funeral and memorial services for non-Orthodox believers, assisting in the composition of these services, which differed only slightly from the Orthodox.

One of the most significant developments in the ecumenical life of the Russian Church was the decision taken on December 16, 1969, by the Holy Synod under the leadership of Patriarch Aleksiy whereby the Holy Sacraments could be administered to Roman Catholics and Old Believers in cases of extreme spiritual necessity. This decision reflected a common faith in the grace-bestowing power of the Holy Mysteries of Christ and was prompted by the Russian Church's concern for the souls of its brothers in Christ.

The next major step in consolidating relations with the Old Believers came with the Local Council of 1971, which lifted the anathema placed on the Old Believers' rites by the Moscow Council of 1656–57. The Council proclaimed that "diversity of external expression does not contradict the redeeming nature of rites," and stated that ancient rites were as efficacious as modern ones. By this act, the Council removed a major obstacle that had prevented the resolution of existing ecclesiastical divisions and the development of good Christian relations with the Old Believers. It also provided a deeper insight into the significance of Church rites, thus furthering the ecumenical movement.

Relations between Moscow and Rome began to grow during the Pontificate of John XXIII (1958–63). The Second Vatican Council, all of whose sessions were attended by theologians from the Russian Church, opened a new era in relations between Catholic and non-Catholic Churches. One of its main achievements was the decree entitled "On Ecumenism and the Pastoral Constitution of the Church in the Modern World."

Contacts with the Vatican are regulated by decisions taken at the Pan-Orthodox Conference at Rhodes (1963 and 1964), which gave every Orthodox Church the right to pursue and develop fraternal relations with the Roman Catholic Church. In the recent years, theologians of both Churches have met together on five different occasions.

Since 1927 the Russian Orthodox Church has cooperated in many areas with the "Pax Christi International," a Catholic pacifist organization. Representatives of the Russian Church attended the Third World Congress of the Apostolate of Catholic Laymen in Rome. Many prominent figures of the Church of Rome have been guests of the Russian Church, visiting its shrines, parishes, cloisters, and schools, with representatives of the Russian Church reciprocating in pilgrimages made to the holy places of the Roman Church. As head of the Department of External Relations, the late Metropolitan Nikodim of Leningrad and Novgorod (1929–78) played a major role in the development of relations between the two Churches. In 1979, his biography of Pope John XXIII was translated into German and published in the Federal Republic of Germany. Contact is now being expanded between lecturers and students of the theological schools in both Russian and Roman Churches. As previously mentioned, several groups of graduates from the Moscow and Leningrad theological schools are now studying at Catholic institutions in Rome, Paris, and Regensburg.

The Russian Church maintains close ties with the ancient Churches of the East, which are known as non-Chalcedonian for their decision not to participate in the Fourth Ecumenical Council of 451 at Chalcedon, thereby alienating themselves from the other Orthodox Churches. In the last century, the Russian Church moved toward a rapprochement by investigating the nature of the theological differences and exploring ways to restore the unity that had been broken fifteen centuries earlier. The Armenian non-Chalcedonian Church maintains particularly close ties—both religious and patriotic—with the Russian Church, inasmuch as its Supreme Patriarch Catholicos is based in Echmiazdin, part of the Armenian Soviet Socialist Republic. The Russian Church also enjoys friendly relations with the Coptic and Ethiopian Churches, the Syrian (Malabar) Church of the East, and the Syrian Jacobite Church. Over the past fifteen years, a number of consultations have been held within the framework of the World Council of Churches between Orthodox and non-Chalcedonian theologians. Members of the Eastern Churches of Armenia, Ethiopia, India, and the Arab Republic of Egypt now study at the theological schools in Moscow and Leningrad, and some have gone as far as defending theses leading to degrees from those institutions.

Contacts with the Anglican Church began more than 250 years ago, but for various reasons the dialogue envisioned at that time did not materialize, and favorable conditions have emerged only in our century. There have been discussions between theologians, as well as reciprocal visits by the Primates of both Churches, all leading to an Anglican-Orthodox Commission. However, difficulties have arisen in the process of rapprochement with certain Anglican Churches that permit the ordination of women—an anathema to the Russian Orthodox Church.

Relations between Russian Orthodoxy and the Old Catholics date back more than a hundred years. Russian theologians were present at the First Congress of Old Catholics that took place in Munich in 1871. In 1892 the Holy Synod formed a commission to consider a reunion between the two Churches. It was only after 1948 that this relationship received new impetus, leading to the Inter-Orthodox Theological Commission on Dialogue with Old Catholics that was set up in 1961. Meetings took place in 1975, 1977, and 1979.

The Russian Church is also in close touch with Lutherans, Evangelists, Methodists, Baptists, and other Reformed Churches. Since mid-century, a dialogue has been developing with the Evangelical Churches of the Federal Republic of Germany, with consultations taking place regularly since 1959. These are known as "the Arnoldstein conversations," after the site of the first meeting. In 1974, Russian theologians met for the first time with the Union of Evangelical Churches, which

represent the majority of Protestant churches of the German Democratic Republic. The meetings that ensued are known as "the Zagorsk conversations." In 1959 a theological encounter took place between representatives of Russian Orthodoxy and those of the Evangelical-Lutheran Church of Finland, which initiated a series of conversations that have continued on a regular basis since 1970. The Lutheran Church of Sweden and the Russian Orthodox Church began their dialogue during the lifetime of that outstanding theologian, Dr. Nathan Soderblom, Archbishop of Uppsala, who corresponded regularly with His Holiness Patriarch Tikhon and other Russian Church hierarchs. Fraternal relations with the Evangelical Lutheral Church of Denmark are expressed in an exchange of high-level Church delegations.

At the first meeting of the Pan-Orthodox Pre-Council Conference in 1976 at Geneva, a decision was taken to set up an inter-Orthodox commission that would include theologians of the Russian Church and have as its purpose the furtherance of dialogue with the Lutherans. The resulting Inter-Orthodox Technical Theological Commission met for the first time in 1978 at Sigtuna, Sweden.

The Russian Church successfully collaborates with the Reformed Churches not only in the ecumenical field but also in mutual efforts to advance the cause of peace. And the Russian Church hopes for a broader interchange with the Methodists following the Thirteenth World Methodist Conference, at which a resolution was made to initiate a fraternal dialogue between Methodists and Russian Orthodoxy.

The Russian Church became a member of the World Council of Churches at its Third Assembly which took place at New Delhi in 1961. Since then, representatives of Russian Orthodoxy have been active in that Council and now serve on various commissions, as well as in departments and sections of its central body. In 1975 Metropolitan Nikodim of Leningrad and Novgorod was elected President at the Council's Fifth Assembly.

The Russian Orthodox Church is clearly aware of the need to do everything possible to assist Christians in achieving unity of faith, in keeping with the commandment of Our Lord Jesus Christ. The Russian Church also strives for social justice and brotherly relations among nations, and tries to further the cause of peace throughout the world. It fully shares the holy aspirations of ecumenism for sincere repentance, renewal, enrichment from the wonders of true faith, and a grace-filled life. Like other Churches, Russian Orthodoxy prays for the restoration of Christian unity within one Holy, Catholic, and Apostolic Church.

The Russian Church meets regularly with the leaders of national and regional Church councils from all over the world. It is in touch with the Lutheran World Federation, the Baptist World Alliance, the World Student Christian Federation, the All-Africa Conference of Churches, and the member Churches of the African and Asian Christian Peace Conference.

The Russian Church has been a charter member of the Conference of European Churches since 1959, and has participated since 1975 in the activities of the Ecumenical Youth Council in Europe, whose goal is the preservation of peace and mutual understanding between the nations of Europe. Indeed, the ecumenical activity of the Russian Orthodox Church is inseparably linked with its efforts in behalf of the most pressing issue of our time: the safeguarding and consolidating of world peace. The Russian Church regards the defense of peace as the fulfillment of Christian duty, and actively pursues this purpose in many different ways. First of all, the Church fervently prays for peace and urges its flock to create peace in their personal lives, honoring the

admonition of Our Lord to " have peace with one another" (Mark 9:50), and pursuing the exhortation of the Apostle to "follow peace with all men" (Hebrews 12:14). Representatives of the Russian Orthodox Church attend all peace conferences in their own country, are active on the Committee for European Security and Cooperation, and support the Peace Fund, which organizes financial support for the public organizations promoting peace among nations. The Russian Church has been active in the Christian Peace Conference since its inception in 1958, and Metropolitan Nikodim of Leningrad and Novgorod was elected President of that organization at the Fourth All-Christian Peace Congress in 1971.

The peace-making ministry of the Russian Orthodox Church encompasses participation in bilateral dialogues with other Churches, such as the meeting in 1979 at Geneva between representatives of Soviet and North American Churches and religious associations. The participants adopted a communiqué entitled "Choose Life," and issued a joint statement urging Christians of the two great powers to work for disarmament.

In its peace-making role, the Russian Orthodox Church cooperates with non-Christian religions. In 1952 his Holiness Georg VI, Supreme Patriarch-Catholicos of all Armenians, convoked the Conference of All Churches and Religious Associations in the USSR. This took place at the Trinity–Saint Sergiy Lavra in Zagorsk at the invitation of His Holiness Patriarch Aleksiy, with the next such conference held again in Zagorsk in 1969. In 1975 His Holiness Patriarch Pimin called another conference to discuss concrete, contemporary problems of peace-making, and he proposed convening a world conference of representatives of Churches and religious associations. The conference convened in Moscow in June 1977, with 663 delegates from

107 countries taking part. Among them were Buddhists, Hindus, Jews, Muslims, Sikhs, Shintoists, and Christians. Together they formulated and adopted the "Appeal to Religious Leaders and Believers of All Religions Throughout the World," which emphasized the importance of intrareligious cooperation in activities related to peace. They also issued an "Appeal to Governments," urging all nations to spread détente throughout the world and extend it to the military and economic sectors. And most recently, Patriarch Pimin addressed the Disarmament Conference at the United Nations in New York City.

The Russian Orthodox Church, in conjunction with the people of the Soviet Union, tirelessly calls not only on Christians but also on all men of good will to take an active part in the great and noble cause of defending peace. The Church regards its work for peace on earth and brotherly cooperation among nations as an indispensable part of Church life and the Christian witness.

163–165 A married parish priest at home in a typical Russian *isba*, a wooden house with carved window frames. In Plate 165 the table is set for a guest.

166 Orthodox priests who are not monks are allowed to have a family, often with a bevy of children whom they bring up to be devoted Christians as well as responsible Soviet citizens. Here we see Archpriest Dimitriy Necvetaet of the Cathedral of the Assumption in Vladimir with his wife and children.

167 Archimandrite Valentin in Suzdal is an energetic parish priest. A collector of church antiques, he is, however, best known as an expert in the old Russian cuisine.

168 Metropolitan Nikolai of Lvov and Ternopol receives his guests for tea in the diocesan community house.

169 Metropolitan Antoniy of Leningrad and Novgorod with his guests at the traditional Russian tea in his *dacha* (country house). As a sign of their dignity, Russian Bishops invariably wear the *enkolipion*, a medallion with the image of the Virgin, for Mary symbolizes the Church whose deputy is the Bishop.

170–180 The Sofrino works near Moscow. This new complex was solemnly opened and consecrated on September 15, 1980. Candles (Plates 171–172), as well as icons and church utensils (Plates 174–177), are manufactured in modern rooms, while some artists paint holy pictures (178–180). The workshops of Sofrino provide the parishes of Moscow Patriarchy with all necessities, as has been the prescribed custom for centuries. In his opening address the Patriarch said to the artists and workers: "May the awareness of the spiritual succession and the wish not only to repeat but to exceed the old masters in beauty and delicacy encourage you to create new works of art."

181 The parish council is always busy with community matters. Here we see the head of the council in conversation with the priest.

182 The arrival of the Metropolitan in a parish is always an important event. Here the faithful crowd around Metropolitan Sergiy of Odessa and Cherson to greet him and receive his blessing.

183 At the beginning of the service the Bishop, in the old Orthodox tradition, stands in front of the eastern pillar, to the right of the sanctuary, in the so-called Bishop's *stasidion*. He wears the *mandyas*, a liturgical garment of Byzantine origin.

184 Before the service the clergy greet their Bishop at the church door. The Bishop blesses them in the church with the cross, and they kiss his proffered hand.

185 Metropolitan Sergiy of Odessa and Cherson on the raised Bishop's seat during the reading from the Acts of the Apostles. Reading from Scripture has always had a special significance in the Russian Orthodox Church.

186 Metropolitan Sergiy kisses the icon of the Virgin Mary of Korsun. Devotion to the Blessed Virgin is characteristic of the Russian Orthodox Church.

187 Metropolitan Sergiy anoints the faithful during a vigil.

188 An Orthodox church contains neither pews nor chairs, and the faithful stand throughout the service. This perpetuates the asceticism of the early Church.

189 The procession of the Cross in the Monastery of the Assumption in Zirovicy on the occasion of the feast of the Zirovicy icon of the Virgin Mary.

190 Metropolitan Filaret of Minsk and White Russia blesses the faithful and the pilgrims during the procession of the Cross.

191 The monastery's *religiae*—a small icon of the Virgin carved from stone—is carried around the church.

192 Rogation services, which are held three days before Ascension, can take place outside as well as inside the church. Here we see an open-air service on the cathedral plaza at the Monastery of the Assumption in Zirovicy.

193–194 Rogation ends with this wish: "For many years!" (*Mnogaya leta!*) On this occasion Metropolitan Filaret blesses the hordes of pilgrims.

195–198 Pilgrims at the Convent of the Assumption in Zirovicy during the feast of the Zirovicy icon of the Virgin Mary. For hundreds of years the Orthodox monks were protectors of the sanctity and safety of prayer, which is of inestimable significance in the Russian Orthodox Church. Every Orthodox Christian believes in the power of a monk's prayer.

199 One further bastion of Orthodox Christianity is the sermon, which here is being delivered in the Cathedral of the Assumption at the Trinity–Saint Sergiy Lavra in Zagorsk. Even today the preacher's words are understood as those of a teacher and father.

200–202 Pentecost at Trinity–Saint Sergiy Lavra in Zagorsk. On this day the faithful and the priest leave the church with consecrated flowers, which they keep at home for the rest of the year.

203 Bishop Athanasiy of Pinsk (left) and Archimandrite Constantin, the Abbot of the Monastery of Zirovicy, take leave of their guest, the photographer Fred Mayer.

165
166▷
167▷▷

181

183

184

195

201

202

203